*For Sol Shenk
and Bébé Wolf*

"David Shenk has written a brilliant confirmation of the fact that information is neither knowledge nor wisdom, and that too much data can dull the mind. One should read this splendid book very soon, while the mind is still intact."
—Roger Rosenblatt

"David Shenk forced me to re-evaluate my longstanding faith in the intrinsic benefits of networking technology. A whole lot of us are crying out for more when we might better be saying 'enough.'"
—Douglas Rushkoff, author of *Media Virus*,
Ecstasy Club, and *Playing the Future*

"A must-read for technophiles and neo-Luddites alike."
—*New York Post*

"Over the past 150 years, humanity solved the problem of information scarcity. In solving it, we created the problem of information glut, incoherence, and meaninglessness. David Shenk's brilliant book names the problem, describes it, explains it, and—God bless him—offers us help in coping with it."
—Neil Postman, author of *Technopoly*
and *Amusing Ourselves to Death*

"[E]legant . . . a blessing . . . Shenk has dealt with his task with a surprising economy of prose and sharpness of wit."
—*Toronto Globe and Mail*

"*Data Smog* offers a rare combination of extensive research, clear thinking, lucid writing, and valuable advice. It's a must for anybody feeling overwhelmed but underserved by today's information sources."
—Edward Tenner, author, *Why Things Bite Back*

"This is a marvelous book." —*Capital Times* (Madison, Wisconsin)

"This book is an oxygen mask. Take it along when you need to breathe. This careful, informed, and passionate argument should take the stuffing right out of the cheerleaders of the (indiscriminate) Information Age."

—Andrei Codrescu, commentator, National Public Radio

"Stunningly eloquent."   —*PC Magazine* Online

"*Data Smog* is quite wonderful . . . a smart warning by a savvy aficionado of cyber-culture to be wary of too much of a good thing."

—Orville Schell, Dean, Graduate School of Journalism, University of California at Berkeley

"A valuable book. . . . If everyone who isn't yet online read *Data Smog* before joining America Online or getting Net access, their lives—and the Net itself—would have a much better shot at staying sane."   —*Salon Magazine*

"This book breaks new ground. Here you will find a public ethic for an era of too much information, delivered in a succinct and heroically civil style that puts to shame an entire shelf of books on the coming media environment. Shenk is a citizen writing for other beleaguered citizens. . . . *Data Smog* is really a book about democracy and what it will take to keep that troubled idea alive and breathing in years ahead."   —Jay Rosen, Director, Project on Public Life and the Press, New York University

"[A] fascinating and important book . . . go and get yourself a copy. Unplug the phone, turn off the TV, and spend a few hours receiving data at a more human speed."   —*Omni Magazine* Online

David Shenk

DATA SMOG

Surviving the Information Glut

REVISED AND UPDATED EDITION

HarperEdge
An Imprint of HarperSanFrancisco

HarperCollins books may be purchased for educational,
business, or sales promotional use. For information please write:
Special Markets Department, HarperCollins Publishers, Inc.,
10 East 53rd Street, New York, NY 10022.

To correspond with the author, e-mail: DataSmog@bigfoot.com

Harper*Edge* Web site: http://www.harpercollins.com/harperedge
HarperCollins®, ☰ ®, HarperSanFrancisco™, and Harper*Edge*™
are trademarks of HarperCollins Publishers, Inc.

FIRST HARPERCOLLINS PAPERBACK EDITION PUBLISHED IN 1998

Library of Congress Cataloging-in-Publication Data
Shenk, David.
Data smog : surviving the information glut / David Shenk.
—1st ed.
Included bibliographical references and index.
ISBN 0–06–018701–8
1. Information society. 2. Information society—United States.
3. Information technology—Social aspects—United States.
I. Title.
HM221.S515   1997   303.48'33—dc21   96–39496

98 99 00 01 02 ❖ RRDH 10 9 8 7 6 5 4 3 2 1

Mr. Mouche climbed on his horse and rode it beautifully.

"You must be proud of yourself," said the professor.

"No," replied Mr. Mouche.

"Still, your horse goes exactly where you want it to go," said the professor.

"That's because I always want to go exactly where the horse wants to go," replied Mr. Mouche.

—Jean-Luc Coudray

Contents

The Laws of Data Smog

1. Information, once rare and cherished like caviar, is now plentiful and taken for granted like potatoes.

2. Silicon circuits evolve much more quickly than human genes.

3. Computers are neither human nor *humane*.

4. Putting a computer in every classroom is like putting an electric power plant in every home.

5. What they sell is not information technology, but information anxiety.

6. Too many experts spoil the clarity.

7. All high-stim roads lead to Times Square.

8. Birds of a feather flock virtually together.

9. The electronic town hall allows for speedy communication and bad decision-making.

10. Equifax is watching.

11. Beware stories that dissolve all complexity.

12. On the information highway, most roads bypass journalists.

13. Cyberspace breeds libertarianism.

DATA
SMOG

> If scientific discovery has not been an
> unalloyed blessing, if it has conferred on
> mankind the power not only to create
> but also to annihilate, it has at the same
> time provided humanity with a supreme
> challenge and a supreme testing.

—John F. Kennedy, 1963

Preface

Something marvelous has been happening to humankind—not just in the last three or four years with computers and the Internet, but more broadly in the last several decades. Information is moving faster and becoming more plentiful, and people everywhere are benefiting from this change.

But there's a surprising postscript to this story. When it comes to information, it turns out that one can have too much of a good thing. At a certain level of input, the law of diminishing returns takes effect; the glut of information no longer adds to our quality of life, but instead begins to cultivate stress, confusion, and even ignorance. Information overload threatens our ability to educate ourselves, and leaves us more vulnerable as consumers and less cohesive as a society. If we're going to make the most of this spectacular information revolution, we need to work hard to counteract these unintended consequences.

This is not the first time we have been confronted by the unpleasant side effects of abundance. We who live in the most sophisticated and successful nation on Earth also routinely find ourselves burdened by problems of excess. Now, for all the wonders technology, a menacing cloud of "data smog" has drifted in. In these pages, we will explore its unwholesome properties and suggest some healthful remedies. This book aims to be a reminder of the critical distinction between information and understanding, and it demonstrates why you don't have to feel personally overloaded with information to be a victim of the information glut. *Data Smog* is also designed to counteract much of the corporate hype surrounding the information revolution. This book is neither techno-utopian nor neo-Luddite. It is *technorealist*—appreciating the benefits of technology while recognizing and responding to its drawbacks.

For clarity's sake, the book is divided into four sections. Part 1, Signal to Noise, reviews the historic transition from information scarcity to information glut, and examines how microtechnology and stimulus overload affect the human animal. How much complexity and information are we designed to handle? When we're flooded with data, what happens to our memories? Our relationships? Our sense of ourselves?

Part 2, Virtual Anarchy, explores the less obvious, but no less serious, social and political consequences of the information revolution—a culture beset by constant "upgrades," a troublesome flood of statistics, an upward spiral of noise, hyper-specialization, and a democracy arguably too "plugged in" for its own good.

Part 3, A New Order, outlines the new power dynamics that arise out of the information chaos. Data smog is an extremely hospitable environment to a medley of unsavory characters and powerful industries. To them, information glut is not a vexing problem, but a fresh opportunity.

Part 4, A Return to Meaning, suggests a path toward a more intelligent tranquillity. Specific government action is suggested, along with a number of personal steps we can all adopt in order to become empowered by information instead of being smothered by it. By taking stock now, perhaps we can help to clear the air and make way for a new information ecology.

PART 1

Signal to Noise

In the information age, there can be
too much exposure and too much
information and too much sort of
quasi-information. . . . There's a
danger that too much stuff cramming in
on people's minds is just as bad for
them as too little, in terms of
the ability to understand,
to comprehend.

—Bill Clinton

chapter 1

Spammed!

I opened the front door and unlocked the iron gate. A man came into my home bearing a prolific new machine, an appliance I mistook to be *generous* in much the same way that people frequently mistake credit cards for currency. It was the infancy of my career as a freelance writer, in Washington, D.C., and somewhere in my enthusiasm for the latest generation of electronic tools, I had gotten the old saw about knowledge and power turned around in my head: I was thinking that *information* was power. I now regard this as one of the great seductive myths of our time and do not feel so silly about falling prey to it; I think it happens to people all the time.

A friend had mentioned this affordable new electronic wire, the Federal News Service, which provided transcripts of key political and cultural events. I felt sure that it would give me a leg up. The pleasant man installed a small off-white printer on a plastic stand on the right rear corner of my desk. Below the stand, he plopped a box of several thousand sheets of perforated paper. He pushed a few buttons to run a test, wished me luck, and was off.

I already had a printer for my computer, of course; this second one stood on its own. It had an antenna in the back, with a small radio transceiver box. Every morning, the printer spat out a roster of the transcripts it had to offer. All the interviews from the morning talk shows, available moments after they had been broadcast. All the major speeches from senators, ambassadors, and other Washington heavies. Absolutely every utterance from the White House. Then it started spitting out the transcripts themselves. A sea of information. I felt plugged in. Without ever leaving my bedroom/office, I felt I had arrived.

Every morning, it printed. And every afternoon. And every evening. And every morning again. In a week, I was running my own private recycling service.

Newsprint was a healthy part of the pile, too. I was reading three papers each morning, along with an abundance of periodicals. Without realizing it, I had at some point made an important (and quite common) strategic decision about how to live in a world that more and more resembles a library without walls, containing more information than one person could ever hope to process. I had decided to confront the rushing tide head on, to try to keep up with the new and speedy, and to more or less disregard the old and slow. I read my newspapers and magazines, my e-mail and my wire services; I watched Cable News Network; I stopped spending time with books and other cumbersome material that felt more like yesterday.

I also listened to talk radio, which is quite good in Washington. One morning on *The Diane Rehm Show,* I heard Diane ask Lewis Lapham, editor of *Harper's* magazine, about the fantastic proliferation of magazines. *It seems you could do nothing but read magazines all day and still not get to all of them,* Diane said at one point. Lewis agreed.

That's weird, I thought. They're talking about me.

At the forefront of the new was my all-too-reliable Federal News Service printer. Somewhere along the line, that empowering eagle became an albatross. One day, it was *so* much; the next, *too* much. -*Uhms* and -*uhrs*, disjointed thoughts, facile questions, and dodgy responses poured into my room morning, noon, and night. Trumped-up charges, non-denial denials, diplomatic rumbles—an entire political universe in dot matrix. The machine also had an unspoken appeal: *keep up*. No one else was around to obey, so it fell to me. The machine expected me to be its equal. It could print two pages a minute—why couldn't I read two pages a minute? Why couldn't I *write* two pages a minute?

The printer had just gone through a dozen transcripts. Was I still working on that same paragraph?

In a month or so, I pulled the plug. The nice man came back and carted the machine away. I locked the gate behind him.

Some years later, in a classroom at Columbia University, I attended a small guest lecture given by Brian Lamb, the founder, chairman, and sometime anchor of C-SPAN, the public-service cable channel that broadcasts congressional debates and other government minutiae. At this talk, Lamb did the most preposterous thing.

He refused to defend the information revolution.

His strange reluctance did not show right away. For an hour or so, Lamb spoke confidently on the history of C-SPAN and why he believed it to be a vital public service. He recalled some of his favorite on-air anecdotes and off-air clashes with important public officials. He boasted of his plans to introduce the new cable channels C-SPAN3, C-SPAN4, and C-SPAN5. After he had finished, his host, Professor Eli Noam, a leading thinker on how information flow affects society, concluded the session by asking Lamb a simple but shocking question. "Is more information necessarily good? Does it really improve the political process?"

En-garde. Noam had questioned Lamb's reason for being. He might as well have slapped him in the face with a white glove and challenged him to a duel. But even more surprising was that Lamb did not spring to the defense of the information revolution, or even the full-access cable channel phenomenon that he had pioneered. Instead, he suddenly and inexplicably surrendered.

"I haven't got a clue as to whether it's good or bad," Lamb replied. "But you can't stop this process. It's the American way. Which part of the library or the Internet do you want to shut down? Let me tell you something: *If we can't survive all the information that we're going to develop, then we're in real trouble.* Because no one is going to stop writing books. No one is going to stop creating information."

How odd those words sounded, coming out of that mouth. Lamb's downcast portrayal of information as an unstoppable steamroller was a complete about-face from his previously boosterish speech about the virtues of the twenty-four-hour government information channel. But I enjoyed the turnaround immensely, because it suddenly revealed Lamb as a much more interesting character than he had earlier seemed—someone who, on one level, at least, grasps the increasingly complex nature of the relationship between human beings and information technology: We thrive on the information, and yet we can also choke on it.

This paradox was something I was still struggling to understand myself. With my fax machine, laptop, and Internet account, I had been lapping up the information revolution as enthusiastically as anyone. I had been training for it, in fact, for most of my life, always fascinated with Radio Shack electronics kits and Casio calculator watches, always believing the next great piece of machinery would take me somewhere new. As a high school sophomore, I spent hours painstakingly writing BASIC computer language to make a green line move from the top of the screen to the bottom on my Apple II Plus (if a$ = "yes" then goto line 20), and back again.

No one within my earshot ever challenged the notion that technology equals progress, so that is what I continued to believe through high school and into my freshman year in college. That year, 1984, I bought one of first generation of Apple Macintosh computers. By the time I graduated, nearly everyone on campus seemed to own one, along with another electronic device that was radically changing the way we communicate: the answering machine.

There were faint whiffs of trouble in the air, but I didn't pick up on them. I can vaguely recall a phone conversation with a college girlfriend shortly after graduation, in which she complained about her office fax machine, yet another appliance sweeping the nation. It wasn't that her fax didn't work, but rather that it was working *too well*. Because it transmitted information across the country and world so quickly, she said, it had actually altered the expectations of work time, becoming a kind of taskmaster that insisted on faster and faster work.

Around this same time, when I was just getting into the journalism business, I got a chance to interview the novelist and social critic Kurt Vonnegut. You can imagine how petrified I was. Just as we sat down to talk in the eat-in kitchen of his midtown Manhattan apartment, my tape recorder died. So much for rechargeable batteries.

Perhaps I should have taken it as a sign that I was beginning my nascent career in exactly the wrong way, with an unhealthy reliance on information technology and not enough confidence in my own faculties. It was Vonnegut himself, after all, who once said, "I began to have my doubts about the truth after it was dropped on Hiroshima." I couldn't see it at the time, but the important thing was the conversation, not in the electro-magnetic tape recording of the conversation. As benign as a tape recorder seems, it is—like almost all technologies—a double-edged sword: While it provides near-perfect reproductions of sound for a cost of next to nothing, it allows one's memory to slip and encourages dependence on the recording.

But as you can probably gather, that wasn't exactly my frame of mind at the time. I could see my big break slipping away, and I could hear my editor telling me not to bother pitching any new stories. Vonnegut took pity and fetched an adapter and an extension cord. We began our business. Throughout the talk, my eyes kept darting nervously back to that red light, the two moving tape wheels.

Early on in our talk, I asked him what was on his current reading list. I guess I expected him to reel off a long list of books, treatises, essays, and so on. Instead, he mentioned one or two items, but mostly just complained of being overwhelmed. He had so many friends who churned out information for a living, he said, he couldn't keep up. "I'm scared to death that someone is going to send me another book," he said.

Ignoring the concerns of these wise people, I turned straight into the head wind. I garnisheed a significant portion of my freelance earnings in order to purchase my own fax machine. Zipping documents around the country at the speed of sound seemed pretty terrific to me. I also upgraded my computer and subscribed to cable television and newspapers and magazines a-plenty. As if that wasn't enough, I then put in a call to the Federal News Service. The man came to my gate with the box . . .

Finally, amidst my own personal information deluge, it began to dawn on me that indeed there might be such a thing as too much information—that, as I would hear Eli Noam suggest much later, more information isn't necessarily better and that, as my ex-girlfriend warned, these machines need to be guarded against as much as celebrated.

When the definitive history of the information revolution is written years from now, one of the milestones will be urban sociologist Richard Meier's warning, in 1962, that society would face a deluge of data within fifty years. Another will be the April 1994 spamming by Canter & Siegel. In Internet jargon, *spamming* is the wanton mass-transmittal of unsolicited electronic messages. (The term is derived from a comedy skit by the absurdist troupe Monty Python in which unsuspecting diners are informed that the restaurant menu includes "egg and bacon, egg sausage and bacon, egg and Spam, egg bacon and Spam, egg bacon sausage and Spam, Spam bacon sausage and Spam, Spam egg Spam Spam bacon and Spam [and so on].") When, in the early 1990s, it was noticed that certain individuals got a kick of out of interrupting text-based Net dialogues with useless and irrelevant drivel, the term "spam" seemed apt.

On April 12, 1994, Laurence Canter and Martha Siegel, a married team of Arizona lawyers, took spamming to an entirely new level of abuse when they posted to over 6,000 Usenet newsgroups an unsolicited commercial offer to help immigrants enter an upcoming "Green Card lottery." (Usenet is a portion of the Internet that provides discussion forums on thousands of specific topics—Japanese animation, the music of Bob Dylan, college basketball, environmental politics, and so on. Archery aficionados from all over the world can stay in touch with one another without regard to geography. Newsgroups are forums for super-specialized dialogue, and off-topic contributions are thoroughly unwelcome.) The international outrage over Canter & Siegel's intrusion—regarded as doubly obnoxious because it was not done in the interests of sharing information but merely to make money—was immediate and overwhelming. So many angry protests were electronically dispatched to Canter & Siegel's Internet service provider that its host computers crashed more than fifteen times. Though the system administrator quickly canceled Canter & Siegel's account, the proud pioneers of major league spamming went on to spam some more, boast about spamming on television, and even write a book (published by HarperCollins, the very same publisher of this book) called *How to Make a Fortune on the Information Superhighway*.

With unsolicited commercial messages—junk e-mail—now showing up in people's boxes every day, it appears that spamming is here to stay. And so, clearly, is the acute sensation (the grating irritation) of being overloaded with unwanted information. The reaction to Canter & Siegel demonstrates that today, many people know—and feel—what Richard Meier warned about thirty-five years ago. Information overload has emerged as a genuine threat.

One certainly does not have to be online to experience it, however. At home, at work, and even at play, communication has engulfed our lives. To be human is to traffic in enormous chunks of data. "Tens of thousands of words daily pulse through our beleaguered brains," says philosopher Philip Novak, "accompanied by a massive amount of other auditory and visual stimuli. In every moment of the audio-visual orgy of our highly informed days, the brain handles a massive amount of electrical traffic. No wonder we feel burnt."

While information overload has surely been accelerated and highlighted by the popularization of the Internet, it is by no means limited to computers or to life in the 1990s. In his 1979 lyrical, fabulist novel, *If on a winter's night a traveler,* Italo Calvino mischievously relates the sensation of being confronted with more information than one knows how to handle:

> In the shop window, you have promptly identified the cover with the title you were looking for. Following this visual trail, you have forced your way through the shop past the thick barricade of Books You Haven't Read, which were frowning at you from the tables and shelves, trying to cow you. But you know you must never allow yourself to be awed . . . but then you are attacked by the infantry of Books That If You Had More Than One Life You Would Certainly Also Read But Unfortunately Your Days Are Numbered . . . you come up beneath the towers of the fortress, where other troops are holding out:
>
> > the Books You've Been Planning to Read For Ages,
> > the Books You've Been Hunting For Years Without Success,
> > the Books Dealing With Something You're Working On At The Moment,
> > the Books You Want To Own So They'll Be Handy Just In Case,
> > the Books You Could Put Aside To Maybe Read This Summer . . .

This is the flip side of what we commonly refer to as our "wealth of information." Information used to be as rare and precious as gold. (It is estimated that one weekday edition of today's *New York Times* contains more information than the average person in seventeenth-century England was likely to come across in an entire lifetime.) Now it is so inexpensive and plentiful that most of it ends up being remaindered and shredded, as if it is worthless garbage.

Therein lies the first great paradox of information glut—we are becoming so information-rich that we take much of what we have for granted. When information wasn't so easily acquired, explains theater director Peter Sellars, "the actual act of finding something had value." But "where there is no pilgrimage, the information itself is debased, devalued and dehumanized. . . . We have everything at our fingertips but we don't value anything."

The First Law of Data Smog
Information, once rare and cherished like caviar, is now plentiful
and taken for granted like potatoes.

Still, the concept of *too much information* seems odd and vaguely inhuman. This is because, in evolutionary–historical terms, this weed in our information landscape has just sprouted—it is only about fifty years old.

Up until then, more information was almost always a good thing. For nearly 100,000 years leading up to this century, information technology has been an unambiguous virtue as a means of sustaining and developing culture. Information and communications have made us steadily healthier, wealthier, more tolerant. Because of information, we understand more about how to overcome the basic challenges of life. Food is more abundant. Our physical structures are sturdier, more reliable. Our societies are more stable, as we have learned how to make political systems function. Our citizens are freer, thanks to a wide dissemination of information that has empowered the individual. Dangerous superstitions and false notions have been washed away: Communicating quickly with people helps to overcome our fear of them and diminishes the likelihood of conflict.

Then, around the time of the first atomic bomb, something strange happened. We began to produce information much faster than we could process it.

This had never happened before. For 100,000 years the three fundamental stages of the communications process—production, distribution, and processing—had been more or less in synch with one another. By and large, over our long history, people have been able to examine and consider information about as quickly as it could be created and circulated. This equipoise lasted through an astonishing range of communications media—the drum, smoke signal, cave painting, horse, town crier, carrier pigeon, newspaper, photograph, telegraph, telephone, radio, and film.

But in the mid–twentieth century this graceful synchrony was abruptly knocked off track with the introduction of computers, microwave transmissions, television, and satellites. These hyper-production and hyper-distribution mechanisms surged ahead of human processing ability, leaving us with a permanent processing deficit, what Finnish sociologist Jaako Lehtonen calls an "information discrepancy."

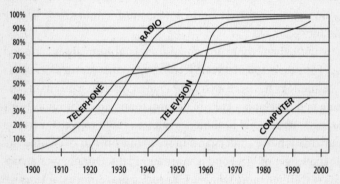

Adoption of information technologies by percent of U.S. population

In this way, in a very short span of natural history, we have vaulted from a state of information scarcity to one of information surplus—from drought to flood in the geological blink of an eye. In 1850, 4 percent of American workers handled information for a living; now *most* do, and information processing (as opposed to material goods) now accounts for more than half of the U.S. gross national product. Data has become more plentiful, more speedy (computer processing speed has doubled every two years for the last thirty years), and more dense (from 1965 to 1995, the average network television advertisement shrunk from 53.1 seconds to 25.4 seconds and the average TV news "soundbite" shrunk from 42.3 seconds to 8.3 seconds; meanwhile, over the same period, the number of ads per network TV minute increased from 1.1 to 2.4).

Information has also become a lot cheaper—to produce, to manipulate, to disseminate. All of this has made us information-rich, empowering Americans with the blessings of applied knowledge. It has also, though, unleashed the potential of information gluttony.

Just as fat has replaced starvation as this nation's number one dietary concern, information overload has replaced information scarcity as an important new emotional, social, and political problem. "The real issue for future technology," says Columbia's Eli Noam, "does not appear to be production of information, and certainly not transmission. Almost anybody can *add* information. The difficult question is how to *reduce* it."

Action photographers often use a machine called a "motor drive" that attaches to 35mm cameras. The motor drive allows a photographer to shoot many separate exposures in any given second just by keeping his or her finger on a button. *Click-click-click-click-click* . . .

What an elegant metaphor for our age: With virtually no effort and for relatively little cost, we can capture as much information as we want. The capturing requires very little planning or forethought, and in fact is built right into the design of our machines. With a thumb and index finger, we effortlessly Copy and Paste sentences, paragraphs, books. After writing e-mail, we "carbon copy" it to one or one hundred others. The same goes for the photocopy machine, onto which we simply enter whatever number of copies we desire. *Would you like those collated and stapled? It's no bother.*

Only as an afterthought do we confront the consequences of such a low transaction cost. "E-mail is an open duct into your central nervous system," says Michael Dertouzos, director of MIT's

Laboratory for Computer Science, exaggerating playfully to make a serious point. "It occupies the brain and reduces productivity."

With information production not only increasing, but *accelerating,* there is no sign that processing will ever catch up. We have quite suddenly mutated into a radically different culture, a civilization that trades in and survives on stylized communication. We no longer hunt or gather; few of us farm or assemble. Instead, we negotiate, we network, we interface. And as we enjoy the many fruits of this burgeoning information civilization, we also have to learn to compensate for the new and permanent side effects of what sociologists, in an academic understatement, call a "message dense" society.

Audio buffs have long been familiar with the phrase *signal-to-noise ratio.* It is engineering parlance for measuring the quality of a sound system by comparing the amount of desired audio signal to the amount of unwanted noise leaking through. In the information age, *signal-to-noise* has also become a useful way to think about social health and stability. How much of the information in our midst is useful, and how much of it gets in the way? What is our signal-to-noise ratio?

We know that the ratio has diminished of late, and that the character of information has changed: As we have accrued more and more of it, information has emerged not only as a currency, but also as a pollutant.

- In 1971 the average American was targeted by at least 560 daily advertising messages. Twenty years later, that number had risen sixfold, to 3,000 messages per day.

- In the office, an average of 60 percent of each person's time is now spent processing documents.

- Paper consumption per capita in the United States tripled from 1940 to 1980 (from 200 to 600 pounds), and tripled *again* from 1980 to 1990 (to 1,800 pounds).

- In the 1980s, third-class mail (used to send publications) grew thirteen times faster than population growth.

- Two-thirds of business managers surveyed report tension with colleagues, loss of job satisfaction, and strained personal relationships as a result of information overload.
- More than 1,000 telemarketing companies employ 4 million Americans, and generate $650 billion in annual sales.

Let us call this unexpected, unwelcome part of our atmosphere "data smog," an expression for the noxious muck and druck of the information age. Data smog gets in the way; it crowds out quiet moments, and obstructs much-needed contemplation. It spoils conversation, literature, and even entertainment. It thwarts skepticism, rendering us less sophisticated as consumers and citizens. It stresses us out.

Data smog is not just the pile of unsolicited catalogs and spam arriving daily in our home and electronic mailboxes. It is also information that we pay handsomely for, that we *crave*—the seductive, mesmerizing quick-cut television ads and the twenty-four-hour up-to-the-minute news flashes. It is the faxes we request as well as the ones we don't; it is the misdialed numbers and drippy sales calls we get during dinnertime; but it is also the Web sites we eagerly visit before and after dinner, the pile of magazines we pore through every month, and the dozens of channels we flip through whenever we get a free moment.

The blank spaces and silent moments in life are fast disappearing. Mostly because we have asked for it, media is everywhere. Televisions, telephones, radios, message beepers, and an assortment of other modern communication and navigational aids are now as ubiquitous as roads and tennis shoes—anywhere humans can go, all forms of media now follow: onto trains, planes, automobiles, into hotel bathrooms, along jogging paths and mountain trails, on bikes and boats . . .

Information and entertainment now conform to our every orientation: Giant television screens adorn stadiums and surround theatrical stages; more ordinary-size TVs hang from ceilings in bars and airport lounges; mini-TVs are installed in front of individual seats in new airliners. Cellular telephone conversation creates a new ambiance for sidewalks and hallways. Beepers and laptop computers follow us home and come with us on vacation.

Meanwhile, the flavor of the information has also changed. It's no longer a matter of mono *versus* stereo or black and white *versus* color. TV and computer screens have been transformed into a hypnotic visual sizzle that MTV aptly calls "eye candy." With hypermedia, "dense TV," and split-screens providing a multiplicity of images at once, straining our attention has become one of our most popular forms of entertainment.

We've heard a lot lately about the moral decay evident in our entertainment packaging. But it isn't so much the content of the messages that should worry us as much their ubiquity, and it is critical to realize that information doesn't have to be unwanted and unattractive to be harmful.

Take advertising (please). Though the bulk of today's commercial messages are aesthetically appealing and can each be considered relatively harmless, in aggregate they have crept into every nook and cranny of our lives—onto our jackets, ties, hats, shirts, and wristbands; onto bikes, benches, cars, trucks, even tennis nets; onto banners trailing behind planes, hanging above sporting and concert events and now, in smaller form, bordering Web pages; onto the sides of blimps hovering in the sky. Magazine ads now communicate not only though color and text but also through smell and even sound.

The smog thickens from the insidious blurring of editorial content and commercial messages in "advertorials" and product placements, to the point where it often becomes impossible to determine whether someone is trying to tell you something or merely *sell* you something. Increasingly, our public spaces are up for rent. "Is it crass?" asks the official marketer for the city of Atlanta, Joel Babbitt, who has designs to sell high-tech advertising on city sidewalks, streets, parks and garbage trucks. "Yes, but so is the Blockbuster Bowl. So is Michael Jordan wearing a Nike cap on the bench and getting a million dollars for it. . . . If it brings in money that helps our citizens, what's the harm?"

What is the harm of an incessant barrage of stimulus captivating our senses at virtually every waking moment? Providing a thorough answer to that question is one of the most important things we can do in our message-dense society, and it is the specific mission of this book.

chapter 2

The Black Shakes

P erhaps the greatest story of acquisition and regret is that of the mythical Greek god Prometheus, whose punishment for stealing fire and passing it down to human beings was to be chained naked to a pillar where each day a vulture tore out his liver. The liver was divinely replenished each night, and the vulture would return to eat it out again the following day. In his dialogue *Protagoras,* Plato puts this story in more contemporary perspective. It wasn't just fire that Prometheus took. It was *techne,* the knowledge of how to make things. The moral is, the price of technological know-how includes a pound of flesh.

Today, the vultures still feed, occasioning a billion-dollar market for antacids like Tagamet and Pepcid AC. For all of our abundance, ours is also an age of unprecedented stress, strain, headaches, and digestive problems—so much so, in fact, that tension has become one of our most vibrant industries. Three out of four Americans complain of chronic stress. Two out of every three visits to the family doctor are thought to be stress-related, and the three top-selling prescription drugs are for ulcers, depression, and hypertension. Stress is also partly to blame, psychologists say, for the startling 300 percent increase in depression over the course of this century.

Stress can have many different sources, of course: financial strain, family pressures, medical problems, and so on. But in a society that has come to be so broadly defined by information technology, it is becoming increasingly clear that the information revolution sweeping us into a new realm of communication is also serving as one of our greatest stressors. Our fast-paced, high-stimulation society leaves many people complaining about being overwhelmed, while many others are becoming unhealthily addicted to the mania. "People seem to be developing a form of Attention Deficit Disorder without inheriting it," says Dr. Theodore Gross, an expert on attention-span disorders. "The information explosion has something to do with it—all the faxes and e-mail and calls come in, and people can't keep up with it."

Attention Deficit Disorder (ADD), an increasingly common brain imbalance, causes acute restlessness and a propensity toward boredom and distraction. Victims of ADD often find it extraordinarily difficult to concentrate on any one thing for more than a few moments. Their minds wander, and they frequently find themselves involved in several things at once.

If these symptoms sound eerily familiar, it is because we may be on the verge of an ADD epidemic. While millions of Americans are thought to suffer from an inherited form of ADD, experts are now seeing a whole new manifestation of what they call "culturally induced ADD." "With so many of these [distracted] people running around," writes Evan I. Schwartz in *Wired* magazine, "we could be becoming the first *society* with Attention Deficit Disorder." Schwartz nominates ADD as "the official brain syndrome of the information age."

Artists have also taken notice of a new high-stim angst. The celebrated off-Broadway theatrical troupe *Blue Man Group* playfully suggests some alternative syndrome names:

Info–Biological Inadequacy Syndrome

A form of anxiety brought on when a person wishes he or she could absorb information at a rate somewhat faster than the level that was hard-wired into human DNA back in the Paleolithic Era.

Fragmentia

A relatively new cognitive disorder where one feels cut off from a sense of wholeness because of common exposure to only in-complete parts of things and ideas which do not—
(The cut-off is intentional).

Perhaps most fittingly, William Gibson, the man who first coined the word and even the very concept of "cyberspace" in his novel *Neuromancer,* also prophesied a nightmarish future of information overload disease called Nerve Attenuation Syndrome, aka The Black Shakes.

No matter how creatively we name it, however, the effects of in-formation overload do not add up to one single debilitating syn-drome that we can easily highlight, recoil in horror from, and muster a simple defense against. A careful review of thirty years of psychological research reveals a wide variety of effects from infor-mation and stimulus overload. A sampling:

- **Increased cardiovascular stress.** Blood pressure rises, leading to strain on the heart and other organs. (Ettema et al., *Ergonomics,* 1971; Boyce, *Ergonomics,* 1974)
- **Weakened vision.** Researchers in Japan have documented an alarming decline in visual acuity from the 1970s to the 1990s, as a result of increased exposure to TVs, VDTs, and other forms of eye-candy. Based on recent trends, a prediction is made that at some point in the not-too-distant future, virtually everyone in Japan will be nearsighted. (Ishikawa, 1995)
- **Confusion.** ". . . consumers [are] unable to effectively and efficiently process the information." (Malhotra, *Journal of Consumer Research*, 1984)

- **Frustration.** ". . . loud speech [and other background noise] lowers frustration tolerance and cognitive complexity . . ." (Rotten et al., *Journal of Applied Psychology*, 1978)

- **Impaired judgment.** ". . . as Information load increases, integrated decision making first increases, reaches an optimum . . . and then decreases . . ." (Streufert et al., *Journal of Experimental Social Psychology*, 1967)

- **Decreased benevolence.** ". . . a person's response to someone needing assistance decreases in likelihood as his environment increases its input bombardment . . ." (Korte et al., *Journal of Personality and Social Psychology*, 1975)

- **Overconfidence.** ". . . as people were given more information, confidence in their judgments increased, but accuracy did not . . ." (Stewart et al., *Organizational Behavior and Human Decision Processes*, 1992)

This last study included a simple diagram illustrating the tapering off and the ultimate decline in accuracy as information increases.

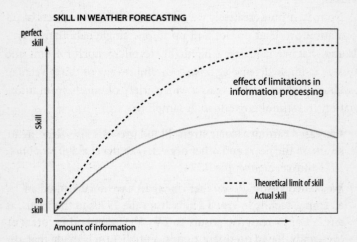

SKILL IN WEATHER FORECASTING

perfect skill

Skill

effect of limitations in information processing

- - - - - Theoretical limit of skill
———— Actual skill

no skill

Amount of information

But perhaps the most important breakthrough in stimulus overload research over the last several decades was the link established in 1970 by psychologist Stanley Milgram to the problems of urban stress. "City life, as we experience it," Milgram wrote in his landmark study, "constitutes a set of encounters with overload, and of resultant adaptations." Those six responses are:

1. Allocation of less time to each input.
2. Disregard of low-priority inputs.
3. Boundaries are re-drawn in certain social transactions so that the overloaded system can shift the burden to the other party in the exchange.
4. Reception is blocked off via unlisted telephone numbers, unfriendly facial expressions, etc.
5. The intensity of inputs is diminished by filtering devices.
6. Specialized institutions are created to absorb inputs that would otherwise swamp the individual.

In 1975 Milgram's hypothesis that sensory overload was the critical factor behind urban distress was confirmed by a study that found it was the level of sensory inputs and not the size of the city that determined how receptive people were to strangers. "Helpfulness shown toward a stranger does not differ between city and town locales," wrote the researchers, "but it is clearly related to the level of environmental inputs."

This validation of Milgram's theory of stimulus overload makes his analysis of overload just as applicable to victims of data smog in 1997 as it was to urban residents of 1970. It also means that as they have faced an unceasing, frequently overwhelming barrage of stimuli in the course of their daily lives, city dwellers have for decades had an excellent preview of the information age in full bloom.

This is bound to be unsettling for those untold millions of Americans who at one time or another have insisted to friends that "New York City is a great place to visit, but I would never want to live there." For these people, who have a visceral reaction against the sensory overload of the big city, information technology arrives with fangs: Regardless of where you live, a virtual rendering of Times Square's hustle and bustle is on its way to your living room and your workplace.

To be sure, high-stim is what city-dwellers are drawn to in the first place. They crowd into cities for *contact* soirees, meetings, news, theater, literature, gossip, and art. So the good news is that this sensory fracas is now largely exportable via television and online technology: voice mail messaging, videophone conferencing, e-mail discussions, and online multi-user "chats." The next generation of magazine stands, online via computer modem (www.enews.com), is now as accessible from a farmhouse in Iowa as it is from my New York City apartment. The speed and breadth of the Net allows for a rapid buzz of social, professional, and intellectual interaction. Acquaintances are made apace, new friendships and even romantic liaisons are formed. On the World Wide Web, we browse through a jumble of academic, artistic, consumer, and media offerings, all equally accessible.

But this is also the bad news. Just as urbanites are also subjected to sirens and horns, squealing brakes, thumps from the ceiling, jackhammers, and random bursts of anger and discomfiting displays of psychosis, so inhabitants of the global skyscraper are facing the ubiquity of media—wanted and unwanted stimuli. As data smog changes the scope of our daily lives, our escapist fantasies evolve. Instead of jaunting off to savor intense new experiences, we design vacations of pure void. An editor friend of mine has just returned from a luxurious Caribbean vacation where, he boasts, he had all the extravagances he desired: no TV, no radio, no newspaper, no computers. "My idea of pure bliss," he says, "is no information at all."

How did we come to a point where our own tools of enlightenment would cause such distress? Ours is a culture of knowledge, an Age of Reason rooted in the sixteenth- and seventeenth-century scientific inquiry of Copernicus, Galileo, and Newton. Communications have been the lifeblood of civilization. But in our roaring technological prosperity, we have, so far, had the luxury to ignore the lesson Marshall McLuhan taught us decades ago: that every technology has "service" effects and "disservice" effects—positive and negative consequences for society.

We are fond of thinking of technology as morally neutral and completely subject to the mores of its human practitioners. But, as Neil Postman explained in his book *Technopoly,* each new tool comes to us with its own particular "embedded ideology." The way we perceive the world around us depends largely on which tool is currently at our disposal. Holding a hammer, one searches for nails; with a knife, one ponders only what to slice; and so on. "Once a technology is admitted [into society]," Postman writes, "it plays out its own hand; it does what it is designed to do. Our task is to understand what that design is." Each technology has its own social agenda—this is also what McLuhan meant by his famous aphorism, "The medium is the message."

We have also ignored, in our arrogance, an important lesson from evolutionary zoology: Though culture moves much more swiftly than evolution, it cannot change the pace of evolution. "For [mankind]," writes popular zoologist Desmond Morris, "the main troubles will stem from the fact that his culturally operated advances will race ahead of any further genetic ones. His genes will lag behind, and he will be constantly reminded that, for all his environment-molding achievements, he is still a very naked ape."

Physically, we are what we are. So while we like to think of humans as adaptable creatures, the plain truth is that because of our complexity and longevity, we aren't nearly as quick to physically adapt as are many other species. In the nineteenth century, the thick smoke from factories in England annihilated white lichens covering tree bark, rendering the previously well-camouflaged white Peppered Moth extremely vulnerable to bird predators. But in just a few years, the previously rare black moths from the same species became dominant, and the Peppered Moth was saved. In recent years, as factory soot has waned in that area and the tree bark has subsequently become light again, evolution has pulled a quick about-face: The moths, too, are white again.

Human evolution, for better or worse, is not so swift; because of this, we may not be able to keep pace with our own technology. Our brains have remained structurally consistent for over 50,000 years, yet exposure to processed information in this century has increased by a factor of thousands (lately, the volume and speed of information has been increasing as much as 100 percent each year). Something has to give.

The Second Law of Data Smog (Cialdini's Law)
Silicon circuits evolve much more quickly than human genes.

"Because technology can evolve much faster than we can," says psychologist Robert Cialdini, "our natural capacity to process information is likely to be increasingly inadequate to handle the surfeit of change, choice, and challenge that is characteristic of modern life."

Psychological tests reveal a bevy of clinical responses to data smog—confusion, frustration, overconfidence, and so on. But what does information overload look like in the real world? For some more personal snapshots of overload experience, I sent out an electronic query on the Internet.

```
Date: Fri, Sep 29, 1995
From: DShenk@aol.com

I'm doing some research on "technostress" for a book on
information overload, and I want to invite comments from
anyone willing to relate some personal experience about
being overrun with data. Dreams, nightmares, memory
lapses, anxiety, and so on. I know I've experienced all of
the above. Have you? If so, let me know your particulars.
```

The response was stunning. From Denmark, Sweden, Germany, Britain, California, New Jersey, Minnesota, and Colorado, I heard from scores of people:

- An accountant who files all of her forms on a computer without any difficulty, but who becomes frozen with indecision when confronted with the open-ended world of the Internet ("There I was, sitting at my computer with the whole world at my fingertips, and it was just too much to deal with. I was paralyzed.")

- A lawyer whose progressive addiction to computers culminated in a terrifying nightmare about being trapped in an endless library.
- A librarian who has been professionally trained to grapple with mountains of information but has lately succumbed to the feeling that the information supply is finally getting out of control.

And a vast assortment of others with memory troubles, sore backs, blurry vision, headaches, and so on. "I experienced cyber-deprivation on several occasions," said one respondent with a self-described addiction to the Net. "Having rest days helps."

One engineer told me he spent so much time debugging software that he began to have recurring nightmares that his mainframe computer was chasing him. A professor at the University of Wolverhampton, in Britain, wrote: "Personally, the speed with which access to information is expanding both terrifies and excites me in about equal measure. One day away from the Net and you feel curious; Two days away from the Net and you feel guilty; three days away from the Net and you're in the stone age."

Another respondent confided that "computer work is like a drug, I cannot give it up."

Indeed, computers, the latest and most powerful engines driving the information glut, have provoked a certain compulsive behavior in a large number of people. The electrifying speed and strobe effect of the computer display monitor can be mildly hypnotic and addictive in the same way that television can, capturing people's attention for long, unhealthy periods of time. I know this from personal experience: the feeling of being driven by the computer to stay *attached*, the manic compulsion to process data as fast and as long as the machine will allow—which is to say, *forever*.

Many computer users also develop feelings of deep dependency on their machines, feeling that they quite literally could not function without them. Philip Nicholson, a researcher specializing in "technostress," demonstrates this regularly in his lectures by posing the following dilemma to each audience: *Pretend that you were forced to make a choice between giving up one of your fingers and giving up use of your computer for the rest of your life.* One-third of the people surveyed choose to give up a finger, Nicholson reports.

Marshall McLuhan said that technologies become extensions of our bodies. Now we know what happens when this phenomenon is taken to its logical extreme. Giving up the computer becomes tantamount to amputation.

Amidst the assortment of testimonials I received via the Net, I discovered the following electronic note:

```
From: BTalty@ultranet.com
To: DShenk@aol.com

David,
I didn't realize that information overload was a phenome-
non that occurs to anyone else, but I recognized it as
soon as I saw the title of your post. I'll share my expe-
rience. I had a nightmare recently that there is just too
much information out there, and I'll never get to all of
it! I woke up with a start, in a cold sweat. The next
morning, when I logged on to the Net (yes, that is the
first thing I do when I wake up—I boot the computer before
I go to the bathroom! Sad, isn't it?) I saw two signature
files on posts that really caught my attention. One was a
quote about a woman whose friends forgot what she looked
like because for the last several years she lived her life
entirely on the Internet. The other was a quote along the
lines of: the desire to know everything is the road to in-
sanity.* Both seemed to relate directly to the feelings in
my nightmare. (And talk about information overload, I see
these things along my surf, and can never remember where I
saw them, or exactly how they went.) . . . Some days I'd
like to move into the woods and become a hermit. (And
bring along only a book or two!)
```

---

* "Insanity is often the logic of an accurate mind overtaxed."—Oliver Wendell Holmes

I also spoke with newspaper editor Samantha Johnson, who a few years ago began spending a lot of her free time—fifteen hours a week or so, in three or four hour stretches—in intense discussions on the Internet. "I felt strangely hyperactive," she says of the physical effect. "I felt like I was in warp speed."

Johnson discovered Usenet through America Online, and was thrilled at the opportunity to interact with thousands of others sharing her interest in Objectivism, the ultra-libertarian philosophy that emerged from the books of Ayn Rand. But soon thereafter, Johnson discovered that one of the unexpected problems of Usenet (and other new media) is that it is so inexpensive and accessible, many newsgroups have become overwhelmed with contributions. Often newsgroups are arguably too popular for their own good.

`Alt.philosophy.objectivism` has thousands of such postings each week, and the expectation is that participants will stay on top of it. "It's impossible to keep up with it," said Johnson, "although we all attempt to do so." Her attempts meant that three or four times a week, four or five hours at a time, she would stare at her computer monitor, scroll through hundreds of posts, read them, respond to them, defend them, and attack them. Her extraordinary effort to *keep up* brought on some unwanted side effects. "I would get out of the chair after being at the computer for a while and have a hard time focusing. I felt dizzy, and I had a difficult time seeing as I'd walk home at night."

Once home, Johnson would have a problem getting to sleep. Her head would spin all night with thoughts of her discussions, and for months she was averaging three or four hours sleep a night. "I was thinking about this stuff over and over, and there was almost no differentiation between what I was thinking and what I was dreaming." The dizziness affected her balance, which threw off her rhythm. As a classically trained dancer, Johnson found these side effects more than simple annoyances. This went on for five months, continuing long after she drastically reduced the number of hours spent on the Net.

When Ezra Pound said that artists are "antennae of the race," he meant that they act as a kind of radar warning system for mankind. The aforementioned information victims are also serving as antennae. They are canaries in our information coal mine.

Add to them *me*, a writer who has long been relying on computers for research, correspondence, and word processing, but with an increasing feeling of unease. Conducting research online from my home office, I have developed a perverse talent for accumulating huge, unwieldy bodies of information on any subject I happened to be researching. For a short column I once wrote on child labor, for example, I was able to download roughly 166 pages of articles on the subject in just a few minutes time—so much material that it was at once a blessing and a burden. On the one hand, I could be relatively sure that somewhere in my data mine were just the nuggets of information I was looking for. But the search itself was oppressive, including the nagging uncertainty that I hadn't found the absolute best material, which stuck with me until I had combed through all the available information.

It is in our nature to leave no stone unturned. But how can one reconcile this dogged determination with an endless field of stones? Researching this book, I naturally have faced the same challenges, which makes for a terrific irony: Here I am writing a book about the information glut, struggling to plow through piles of information on the subject of information. I am both researcher and participant, lab technician and lab rat.

By way of illustration, here is a summary of what I've collected over four years of research. I have:

- purchased 40 books
- photocopied 600 pages from library books and journals
- torn out 575 newspaper and magazine articles
- recorded 80 hours of interviews

These numbers are normal and will not surprise anyone who has done a large research project. But my electronic access has brought me a mountain of information that has dwarfed my conventional research material. Electronically, I have:

- conducted 481 NEXIS searches, downloading 46.2 megabytes (the equivalent to 14,000 pages) of text.
- visited roughly 1,000 Websites, downloading hundreds of additional pages of text.

All told, I have electronically amassed 700 separate text files, taking up 69.2 megabytes of memory space on my computer—that's 69 million "bytes," the equivalent of 23,067 pages of text. My master notes file alone contains 240,000 words, the equivalent of about 1,000 pages.

From the computer's perspective, this is all entirely manageable. But in human terms, it is burdensome. Information that starts out looking like a useful set of tools soon winds up resembling an overstocked hardware store. Instead of spending time using my tools, I am forced to waste time organizing them and then combing through them. My huge notes file is accessible by technical means, but for practical purposes it is virtually inaccessible to me, except by key-word search. Browsing through my electronic notes with any degree of diligence would take months.

In the age where information has become our most valuable commodity, I have become an information Midas. Like the King who was granted his thoughtless wish that everything he touch turn instantly into gold, only to discover that he could no longer eat or drink, I have found that, because of my electronic access, nearly everything I touch turns into digital information, to be downloaded and stored on the internal hard drive of my laptop computer. But what is this "wealth" really worth?

I now realize that it is only as valuable as it is useful.

The e-mail from BTalty@ultranet.com included a complaint about memory loss: "I see these things along my surf, and can never remember where I saw them, or exactly how they went." For anyone immersed in data smog, this has a very familiar ring. It calls to mind the doctor who heard of many complaints of people losing their memory, wondering if they were developing some horrible malady. "They are not in a stage of early Alzheimer's," he concluded. "They've just got so much information coming in at once that the mind can't process it all."

I've certainly noticed a problem with my own memory, and have had countless conversations with others as they tried to recall in vain where they came across some specific piece of information. "We're exceptional at storing information," explains UCLA memory expert Robert Bjork. "But there are retrieval limitations. We get overloaded. We know the name of that high school friend. It is in our memory somewhere, but we can't quite get to it." The specific culprit involved in our increasingly spotty memories, he says, is "cue overload." Memory is stored according to specific cues—contexts within which the information is experienced. You are reading *The Right Stuff* in a rocking chair in your lamp-lit living room, listening to the Oscar Peterson Trio. You are having a conversation about ESPN over a cabbage and cilantro salad. These events are recorded in your brain as a team of integrated thoughts, images, and observations. Thinking of one might well trigger a recall of the other. The ESPN memory will always bring some of the restaurant context along with it.

The problem comes when the contexts begin to vanish in the sea of data. Perhaps, like me, you now read nearly everything off the same computer screen, in the same sitting position, in the same spot in the same room. Perhaps the majority of your conversations now take place over the same phone in the same chair. "When many different things get associated with the same situational cues," explains Bjork, "you're going to have a greater difficulty remembering any one of those things. With information overload, retrieval becomes more difficult."

Here is a demonstration of what Bjork calls the "List-Link Law." Read out each of the letters and numbers from group one to yourself.

Then close your eyes and recite from memory.
2H9.

Now try the same thing with group two:
47Q93F.

Now try the same thing with group three:
8J3, D67, NVB, WS4, 2W9A, 11OL.

Now the same with group four:
N4214, NFBC, ZYTV, GFM, 85UY, 9K1L, 459O, IL1, 77H, 84CV, DWS3, AEB4, EBRK, EAR6, 811I.

Clearly, it gets harder and harder to remember the whole list as the lists get longer. But more important, it becomes more difficult to remember *any single piece of it.* "The more things there are on a list to remember or to learn," explains Bjork, "the lower the probability that you'll remember any one of them. It just overloads the system."

The loss of context can have emotional ramifications as well. Marshall McLuhan warned us about taking the mind out of the body, speeding it up, and giving it the ability to float into the electronic void. He called this the Discarnate Effect. "We're pushing ourselves to speeds beyond which it appears we were designed to live," says Nelson Thall, director of research at the University of Toronto's Marshall McLuhan Center. "Man wakes up today and electric technology speeds up his mind to an extraordinary degree, but his body stays in place. This gap causes a lot of stress. Your mind is empowered with the ability to float out into the electronic void, being everywhere at once. You are no longer flesh and blood." In our increasingly virtual existence, physical borders that for tens of thousands of years have helped define who we are are fast becoming obsolete. We can "go" almost anywhere at any time, in the virtual world. Our options are no longer limited by money or distance—only by time.

BS! NOT EVERYONE (MOST DON'T) HAS A PC + THOSE W/ PCS CAN'T GET LEXIS-NEXUS AFFORD

But this new surfeit of choice also threatens our identities, our spiritual selves. In *Zen And the Art of Motorcycle Maintenance,* Robert Pirsig offers a practical solution to the existential alienation people suffer in modern society: His prescription is for people to reattach themselves to the technologies that they depend on by learning how they work. As "sophisticated" as we are, he argues, we still need to feel connected to our world in a rudimentary way. But Pirsig's ideas, as sound as they are, are becoming obsolete. As the sophistication of the machinery increases each year, his solution of reattachment is increasingly unavailable to us. Sadly, we're creating a world so complex that each of us will understand less and less about it. In the advanced stages of "Info-biological Inadequacy Syndrome," life itself is increasingly a mysterious bag of tricks that most of us are left to gawk at from the peanut gallery—entertained, perhaps, but thoroughly detached from the events on stage.

chapter 3

Skeptical in Seattle

The unintended consequences of information technology

The sun is beginning to go down over Lake Washington, in Seattle. The clouds that have been hovering all day (all week, all month) fold into each other like fingers from oversized gloves, and hang over the vast lake with gloomy resolve. Following directions scratched out on a business card at a pay phone, I snake down a hilly driveway in my bronze rental car. My host, K., greets me. After many faceless phone conversations, here at long last are two eyes to look into, a hand to shake. Inside, I cautiously remove a microcassette recorder from my coat pocket, trying to nudge him to finally speak on the record. Just as I had feared, a tight grimace takes hold of his face. "I'd rather not," he says in a familiar tone. "I'm going to be a lot less candid with that thing on."

For the sake of my own enlightenment, then, anonymity will have to suffice. K. will remain "K." We step out back onto a brick patio and down the terraced lawn to a private wooden pier stretching into the murky green water. Thankfully, the clouds do not shroud majestic Mt. Rainier, the mammoth, 14,410-foot glimmering glacier just a few miles away. Across the lake, a more contemporary monument for the region is being installed: Microsoft chairman Bill Gates's $30 million palace of interactive wonder. To hear Gates boast, it is not so much a house as it is a hallowed shrine of technology, a temple of silicon worship. Here is the house whose electronic walls will automatically adjust art, music, temperature, and lighting, according to the tastes of each guest.

Down the way, also on the lakefront, is the home of Keith McCaw, one of the four brothers who sold Cellular One to AT&T for $4 billion. Spread out around town, in fact, are a handful of software billionaires and thousands of industry millionaires (more than 2,000 from Microsoft alone). People feel good about the information revolution in these parts, and why shouldn't they? Microsoft and its neighboring corporate cousins account for more than $7 billion in annual revenue, a healthy portion of which sustains parks, roads, and the general welfare and happiness of Washington's citizens.

When Bill Gates promises, in his book *The Road Ahead,* that the information superhighway will bolster democracy, spread educational advantages to even the poorest kids, and usher in a world of "low-friction, low-overhead capitalism . . . a shopper's heaven," he has more than seductive sales jargon and hypnotic TV commercials backing him up. He also has a cheerleading squad that includes millions of gratified Seattleites and, not incidentally, an unprecedented consortium of corporations—Baby Bells, cable companies, TV networks, publishers, software producers, hardware manufacturers, advertising agencies, entertainment moguls, and video game companies. All are eagerly shifting resources onto the information superhighway as the dynamic new engine promising to drive economic growth for the next century. *Did you ever give your baby an algebra lesson from a thousand miles away? You will.* Corporate America can't wait to bring it to you. The information superhighway is expected to generate $1 trillion in annual revenue by the year 2000, making it the largest industrial sector in the world.

K. is not sold, though. He knows Bill Gates and many of t'
other bigwigs personally—he's one of them, in fact, having a'
made a small fortune in the industry. But even as a senior executive
at a major software company, he is not sanguine about the social
consequences of advanced technology. As he sees it, the road ahead
is paved not with prosperity and democratic virtue, but with cata-
clysm. "This is like the atom bomb," he says. "People just don't understand how tumultuous this technological revolution is going to
be. They think that the world will look pretty much the way it does
now, just *faster*. But they don't get it: It's going to be a completely
different world. I'd say democracy has about a fifty-fifty chance of
survival."

K. fears that information technology, for all of its conveniences,
is also dragging down the level of our discourse; and that in the increasing pace and distraction of our informationized culture, our
two centuries of democracy will fall prey to demagogues. As a student of history, he knows that this has happened before. Radio
brought Franklin Roosevelt into millions of American homes and
strengthened a sense of national resolve in an era of great crises. But
the 1930s also saw Hitler and a host of other demagogues sweep into power on the wings of the same technology. Television did not
become the educational panacea that many confidently assumed.
Instead, it boosted the careers of Jimmy Swaggart, Pat Buchanan,
and other "great communicators," and has played an important role
in degrading education and politics in this country. The great propagandists of our time have understood better than anyone else the
power of communications technology, and one need only look at a
few television advertisements to affirm that this is still true today.

K.'s insistence on anonymity, then, is not out of bashfulness.
Attribution could cost him his job, or worse. One thing might lead
to another, stocks could plummet, careers and companies could un-
ravel, and so on. But the story is important, and he seems compelled
to tell what he knows.

K. is not the only one to worry about the legacy of this technology. There is a mostly unspoken but still acknowledged anxiety and
ambivalence regarding technology that bleeds right into advertising.

In one magazine ad for IBM, an exhausted office worker puts both hands over his face. Lines of text are pasted over his pose of exhaustion:

> Marketing says, "Get me quick turnaround." . . .
> Your brain says, "Get me out of here."

In a similar vein, a television commercial for Volkswagen has a young, vibrant narrator boasting:

> I've got gigabytes. I've got megabytes. I'm voice-mailed. I'm e-mailed. I surf the net. I'm on the Web. I am Cyber-Man. So how come I feel so out of touch?

Even *Wired* magazine features ads that simultaneously celebrate and subconsciously lament the frenzied information superhighway lifestyle. One such ad for the NEC Multispin 6X CD-ROM drive shows excruciating photographs of a man experiencing multiple G-forces on his face.

The Japanese ivy *Kudzu* also comes to mind, as does the Australian *Melaleuca* "punk" tree. Early in this century, both species were eagerly imported into regions of the U.S. as ecological white knights—*Kudzu* to stop erosion in the Tennessee Valley, *Melaleuca* to drain swamp land in Florida. The problem is that *Kudzu* and *Melaleuca* do not particularly care about topsoil or the economics of farming. They have their own interests to attend to. Both plants flourished to such an extent that their successes became a brand new ecological problem for each region. Now, decades later, both are regarded by humans as biological terrorists, with *Kudzu* asphyxiating the dogwood, white oak, and Carolina red maple in Tennessee and surrounding states, while *Melaleuca* has devoured a preposterous 450,000 acres of the Florida Everglades, and is still on the rampage at a clip of fifty acres a day.

Similarly, all technologies introduced into our human ecosystem come with a raft of expected and unexpected consequences. Just as automobiles have not only been a great force of liberation and convenience but also one of our most dangerous polluters and most reliable sources of injury and death, we are now facing many unexpected, unwelcome ecological hazards out on the information highway. Even as computers help fuel an age of immense commercial, cultural, and political possibility, they also contribute to skyrocketing levels of stress and depression, a dangerous fragmentation of culture, a stimulus-dense society with fewer and fewer escapes, dangerous use of database technology; and a hyper-cut, hypnotic, "dense TV" that renders television an even less socially progressive tool than before.

Perhaps the least welcome consequences of our current revolution will come out of our increasing interconnectedness—our *webness*. As an indicator of the extent of our vulnerability, one survey reveals that, in one sixty-day period in 1996, half of all large North American companies suffered damage from a computer virus. Like real biological viruses, computer viruses cause equal parts justifiable paranoia and physical damage. "With computer networks, [vandals] have an amplifying effect that they've never had before," admits Eric Schmidt, chief technical officer at Sun Microsystems. "If I were a criminal with a gun, I might attack one person. But with a computer network, I can attack a million people at a time. It's like an atomic bomb."

Again, someone in the industry has compared the information revolution to the atomic bomb. We can't shake the eerie sensation that we are losing control to the very machines that were supposed to serve us. "Chaos is upon us," says the Electronic Frontier Foundation's John Perry Barlow. "Every single stable power relationship is going to be called into question by cyberspace."

This is not the first time that machines have helped to set the agenda, of course, but a Rubicon does appear to have been crossed. Inevitably, these concerns all come back to Neil Postman's contention that machines rarely have the same ambition as their inventors, that they play out their own hand, and that our task is to figure out what that is, rather than simply hope for the best.

In the 1960s, labor experts were forecasting that the computer revolution would quickly lead to a four-day, thirty-two-hour work week. "Everyone expected that technology would automatically deliver us from work," says Harvard economist Juliet Schor. "[The experts] thought what we'd be talking about today would be a crisis of leisure time . . . that boredom would be the big problem facing the American people." Needless to say, it didn't quite work out that way. As Schor reports in her book *The Overworked American,* we are now working 164 hours *more* per year than we did twenty years ago—the equivalent of one extra working month each year.

How did this happen? "Technology reduces the amount of time it takes to do any one task," explains Schor, "but also leads to the expansion of tasks that people are *expected* to do. This is what happened to American housewives over the twentieth century as they got new household appliances. They didn't actually do less work—they did more things. It's what happens to people when they get computers and faxes and cellular telephones and all of the new technologies that are coming out today."

In essence, then, computers are our modern *taskmasters,* constantly picking up the pace. When humans can't keep up in certain tasks, computers simply replace people altogether. "If you don't have the right skills," warns former Labor Secretary Robert Reich, "technology may be your enemy."

The Third Law of Data Smog
Computers are neither human nor *humane.*

Put simply, computers aren't human. Consequently, the more we rely on computers to answer telephone calls, the more we wind up in what *we* consider "voice mail hell." To the machine, it doesn't matter whether you're in an endless loop. So even as we benefit from the computer's ability to supervise complex tasks, we will also face the consequences of letting it make important decisions: machines will more and more be at the center of power and phone outages, toxic gas leaks, plane crashes, and other social breakdowns. (One forum on the Internet, called "RISKS," is dedicated completely to the unintended consequences of technology.)

Perhaps the most prominent example of this phenomenon emerging now is the year-zero problem. Since the vast majority of computers in use today use only two digits to signify the year, they are unable to compute years beyond the 1900s. This means that any year after 1999 is currently read as early twentieth century. A computer computes 2001, for example, as 1901. What at first blush seems like a trivial problem becomes almost farcically large, considering the implications and considering the cost of the fix—an estimated hundreds of millions or even billions of dollars worldwide. Everything associated with a date, from social security checks to committee rosters to revenue estimates to court dockets, will be affected. "There are going to be some governments that come crashing to their knees when their computer systems fail," says computer consultant Jack Townsend. The year-zero problem has already spawned a cottage industry of software entrepreneurs aiming to fix it in the cheapest and easiest way possible.

The extent of the year-zero problem is indicative of how dependent we have come to be on our machines, and how much we have to conform our lives to their dynamics. Yet our infectious optimism thrives, partly because it is in our nature to be doggedly optimistic. This determination to live out our childlike fantasy that blind devotion to technology will guarantee benefits without drawbacks is called "technological utopianism." It is in this spirit that we continue on, inviting computers into our every domain. Pretending that they conform to our world, we actually adapt to theirs, accepting increasing complexity in our lives for better or worse.

chapter 4

"A New Generation of Geniuses"

Dreaming the techno-utopian dream

David Sarnoff, the founder of NBC and the man who unveiled the first color television at the New York World's Fair in 1939, was one of the great techno-utopians of the twentieth century. What would he think of his creation now? We can only surmise what would happen if he came back today, settled in a comfy chair, and learned to surf through the fifty-some-odd channels of raunch, indiscriminate violence, and solicitous banality propped up by laugh tracks that now pass for televised entertainment. I think it's likely that he would sit and stare, mouth agape. With a pained expression he would slowly turn to the others in the room and ask, *What the hell happened?*

Like many others, Sarnoff saw the new invention not as the "idiot box" of today, but as a force for truth, refined culture, and national edification. In 1940 he declared confidently that television was "destined to provide greater knowledge to larger numbers of people, truer perception of the meaning of current events, more accurate appraisal of men in public life, and a broader understanding of the needs and aspirations of our fellow human beings." Sarnoff made a number of efforts to put these ideals into practice. In the late 1930s, for example, he established the NBC Orchestra, recruiting the world-renowned Arturo Toscanini to conduct weekly radio and then televised concerts in prime time.

Although edifying programming like this still exists, television's greatest influence has been at the other end of the spectrum, promoting voracious consumerism, political apathy, and social isolation. We are not knowledge seekers when we watch TV; we are couch potatoes. Sarnoff saw television as our modern Agora, where as a nation we could come together to share in modern virtue and progressive democracy. Instead, it has become our Coliseum, where we all come together to watch others get torn apart.

Today's children, who watch more television than ever before (an average of 22,000 hours before graduating from high school), according to the *Washington Post*, also "suffer from an epidemic of attention-deficit disorders, diminished language skills, and poor reading comprehension." The U.S. Department of Health and Human Services has discovered a direct link, and there is concern that TV might actually cause learning disorders. "Most [heavy-viewing] kids," says psychologist Jerome Singer, "show lower information, lower reading recognition or readiness to reading, [and] lower reading levels." They also "tend to show lower imaginativeness and less complex language usage." Very recent research in this field suggests that TV might in fact physically stunt the growth of a developing brain.

The great lesson is, beware of men bearing magical machines and a list of hopeful prophecies attached. Beware, for instance, of Microsoft Chairman Bill Gates's assertion: "I expect education of all kinds to improve significantly within the next decade . . . information technology will empower people of all ages, both inside and outside the classroom, to learn more easily, enjoyably, and success fully than ever before."

This sort of mindless techno-utopianism threatens to distract us from a more rational examination of the actual consequences of various technologies. But because it is a wonderfully seductive fantasy that is so difficult for Americans to resist, it is employed again and again by would-be visionaries. Ever on the horizon sits a wondrous technology promising to deliver a truly equitable, educated, civil democratic society. And, though it never does quite work out that way, the hope springs eternal.

The most elegant description I have seen of this blind faith is in a collaboration of French pop artist Moebius and writer Jean-Luc Coudray, from Coudray's book, *Stories of Mr. Mouche.*

Mr. Mouche climbed on his horse and rode it beautifully.

"You must be proud of yourself," said the professor.

"No," replied Mr. Mouche.

"Still, your horse goes exactly where you want it to go," said the professor.

"That's because I always want to go exactly where the horse wants to go," replied Mr. Mouche.

I have no idea whether or not Coudray or Moebius intended any technological reference at all; but in any case, theirs is a dead-on depiction of techno-utopianism: Wherever technology may lead us, we're happy to go along for the ride. As a part of our rugged, can-do spirit, we stubbornly refuse to abandon the reckless faith that an emerging generation of machines will lessen all woes.

 Most dangerously, techno-utopianism allows us to take our minds off the problems themselves, and off the need for now-un conventional, nonelectronic solutions.

Even more than David Sarnoff, there is another ghost I wish I could summon to the present. I can't help but wonder how Vannevar Bush would feel sitting at my own desk in Manhattan and exploring my Macintosh Powerbook 180 computer as a gateway to a strange and exciting virtual world—sending electronic mail halfway around the globe and receiving a reply within minutes; searching millions of pages of formatted text with key words and phrases, electronically sorting and editing documents at will.

How fantastic and utterly terrifying: his prophecies *all realized.* In July 1945, Bush, director of the wartime Office of Scientific Research and Development and the "superbrain" overseer of the Manhattan Project, published an article in *The Atlantic Monthly* entitled, "As We May Think." It laid out the future of information technology in striking detail. In eight pages, Bush outlined the concepts of microfiche, modems, fax machines, personal computers, hard drives, voice-operated word processors, and, most important, *hypermedia.* He imagined the future work desk—a "memex," he called it—as a micro-library filled with all the video and text that one person could accumulate in a lifetime, designed with the ability to retrieve relevant information instantaneously and project it onto a built-in display terminal. As one conducted research and discovered new pathways between parcels of data, new electronic links would be forged that would enable one's trail to be retraced in the future.

"The human mind," he wrote, "operates by association. With one item in its grasp, it snaps instantly to the next that is suggested by the association of thoughts, in accordance with some intricate web of trails carried by the cells of the brain. . . . Man cannot hope fully to duplicate this mental process artificially, [but] selection by association, rather than by indexing, may yet be mechanized."

Bush's confidence in the virtue of technology was consistent with a long tradition of American technical optimism. Coming at the height of American achievement in World War II, it was also perfectly suited to the time. American military technology had saved the free world, the thinking went, and now its domestic technology would swiftly improve the lives of all Americans. It became the foundation of the American economic recovery from the Depression that preceded the war—a recovery that was by no means considered certain at the time.

It is difficult to imagine now, but as recently as 1945, capitalism was still considered a rocky American experiment. Memories of the Great Depression still stung, and anxiety about America's economic future was high. Today we take that famous post–World War II boom of industry, consumerism, and baby-making for granted. But back then, political and economic leaders were not at all sanguine. In fact, another economic depression was widely expected.

To prevent this imminent collapse, it was also widely felt, a great new resource had to be discovered and tapped. According to Frederick Jackson Turner's popular "frontier thesis," economic expansion depended on finding a replacement for the dwindling supply of undeveloped western land. In July 1945, Bush boldly named that precious new resource: *information.* The same month that his *Atlantic Monthly* article appeared, he also presented President Harry Truman with "Science—The Endless Frontier," a report recommending the creation of a National Research Foundation. "Without scientific progress," Bush wrote, "no amount of achievement in other directions can insure our health, prosperity, and security as a nation in the modern world."

So emerged the postwar zeitgeist of techno-utopianism. It was not a question of *whether* information technology would improve society, only *when*. A startling, invigorating, enlightening information revolution was on its way. Indeed, the machines came—the photocopier, telex, magnetic recording tape, cable television, computer, fax, fiber optics, and the Internet. Right here on my desk is that very electronic "web" that Bush wrote about, a portion of the Internet known, in fact, as the World Wide Web, where I move freely from multimedia page to multimedia page with simple clicks of the mouse, blazing a unique electronic data trail and keeping a record of my path.

As Bush prophesied: "The lawyer has at his touch the associated opinions and decisions of his whole experience, with familiar trails to every point of his client's interest. The physician, puzzled by a patient's reactions, strikes the trail established in studying an earlier similar case, and runs rapidly through analogous case histories, with side references of the classics for the pertinent anatomy and histology. The chemist . . . "

There were other dreamers of this golden dream. Today's World Wide Web surfers are enjoying not only the fruition of Bush's hyperlinked, hypermedia memex, but also that of the "Noosphere," an electronic convergence of world consciousness conjured up around the same time by French theologian Pierre Teilhard de Chardin; and the electronic "World Brain," an authoritative, continually updated world encyclopedia of knowledge proposed a few years earlier by science fiction writer H. G. Wells.

Here it is, everything these visionaries asked for, and then some. And yet I'm certain that something about these developments would not feel quite right to the visionaries. For they also felt sure that these miraculous machines of the future would, in a substantial way, raise humankind onto a higher plane of existence—"elevate man's spirit," as Bush phrased it. "They may yet allow [humankind] truly to encompass the great record and to grow in the wisdom of race experience," he wrote. Similarly, Teilhard de Chardin spoke of his Noosphere as a network of "super-organization of Matter upon itself . . . the liberation of consciousness." Wells envisioned a "standing editorial organization" that "would be the mental background of every intelligent man in the world. It would be alive and growing and changing continually under revision, extension, and replacement from the original thinkers in the world everywhere."

As fantastic as the Web is, it is none of these things. To be sure, there is a vast supply of scattered intelligence, much of it breaking new ground aesthetically and intellectually. But there is also much of the old, problematic world thrown into the mix. Like our physical mail boxes, our e-mail boxes are stuffed with electronic junk sales pitches from hucksters. Indiscriminate violence exists in the form of computer viruses (so prevalent that several new viruses are now created every day). Pornography is also rampant. The virtual world has turned out to include all of the unsavory elements of the physical world.

The information tools that yesterday's techno-utopians dreamed about have arrived, but the machines are not the cultural panaceas they had prophesied. This is perhaps best evidenced by knowledge surveys. Though we have experienced a vast democratization of education over the last fifty years (in 1940 only 38.1 percent of the population had completed high school; by 1990 that figure had climbed to 85.7 percent), there has not been anything close to a concurrent rise in social knowledge. "The ultimate irony of [our] findings," wrote pollster Andrew Kohut in a 1990 survey report for the Times Mirror Center for The People & The Press, "is that the information age [has] spawned such an uninformed and uninvolved population."

This stark reality clashes with what many in Washington, D.C., cheerily continue to refer to as our "well-informed citizenry." A few years ago, I paid a visit to then–Federal Communications Commission (FCC) Chairman James Quello, to ask him about his recent use of that phrase. "I think everyone'll agree we're probably the best-informed people in the world," he said. "We have a lot of news and public affairs ... and the public is getting more sophisticated. Maybe ten or twenty years ago, you could pull the wool over our eyes. But not now."

A decorated World War II veteran who served in infantry divisions in North Africa and Europe, Quello afterward had gone into the broadcasting business. Since 1974 he had been on the other side of that fence, vested with helping to protect the public's interest in phone lines, radio waves, and TV transmission. As the recently appointed FCC chairman, this octogenarian who'd been around before the first transcontinental telephone call was now a key player in laying the foundation for America's information superhighway.

I told Quello that my research seemed to call his assumptions into question. In a 1986 survey, for example, in which Americans were asked to identify the particular government jobs held by George Bush, Tip O'Neill, Caspar Weinberger, William Rehnquist, Paul Volcker, and Bob Dole:

- 4 percent of the respondents could name the positions of all six.
- 5 percent knew five.
- 8 percent knew four.
- 17 percent knew three.
- 26 percent knew just two.
- 21 percent knew only one.

- *and 19 percent missed all six.*

"No fooling?" he said. "Where in hell did they take this—in the backwoods of Kentucky or Tennessee?" (Quello is from Detroit, Michigan.)

I told him no, these were national polls, a random sampling of American adults. I read him another one. "In a survey of 2,100 college students on forty different campuses," I began—

"College students? They did a little better, I hope?"

Not really. Two-fifths of them thought that prehistoric people had to protect themselves from dinosaurs, thoroughly unaware of the 65-million-year span between the last dinosaur and the first human being.

He started to fidget a little. "Maybe we need an [improved] educational process," he said. "There's only one trouble with educational TV—it gets turned off for sports or entertainment. I don't know what we can do about that."

I continued. "In 1986 the question was, 'To the best of your knowledge, during World War II, was the Soviet Union ever an ally of the United States—?'"

"*Oh my God,*" he said in anticipated dread.

"A third did not know we were ever allies."

"Now, World War II," he said. "I would think history class would take care of that somehow."

I decided to finish up with something more contemporary. I asked if he recalled the controversy during the Persian Gulf war about whether the United Nations should pressure Kuwait to become more democratic.

Sure. Of course he remembered that. It was an enormous issue.

At the height of that controversy, a poll was taken. "Question: To the best of your knowledge, does Kuwait have a democratic or undemocratic system of government?"

- 52 percent weren't sure.
- 6 percent thought Kuwait already was democratic.
- Only 42 percent knew that Kuwait was not democratic.

The chairman was incredulous. "You had a better chance of answering right if you guessed! There's so much news and news analysis about," he said. "It seems to me that if people would just tune in, they'd be better informed than that."

This dichotomy between data and knowledge, between publicly available information and public understanding, has baffled experts for years. In 1989 political scientist Eric Smith tried to record the assumed rise in public knowledge corresponding to the dramatic expansion in public education over this century—but he couldn't find it. So he wrote a book called *The Unchanging American Voter.*[*]

---

[*] "Americans' *innocence* of political knowledge has been so thoroughly documented that it is no longer noteworthy," wrote Smith's peer Stephen Bennett, grading Americans "a resounding 'F'" on political knowledge. Bennett also concluded that there had been virtually no improvement from dismal knowledge surveys over a period of forty years, and that "the analysis here casts serious doubts about the 'improvability' of mass publics, which is one of the tenets of the citizenship theory of democracy."

After a steady series of breakthroughs in information technology, we are left with a citizenry that is certainly no more interested or capable of supporting a healthy representative democracy than it was fifty years ago, and may well be less capable. This is a stark contrast to the luxurious promises of the techno-utopians. At best, our advanced technology has had a mixed social and political legacy.

Yet, like the cockroach and the common cold, technological utopianism perseveres. Twenty years ago, Xerox ran advertisements featuring Brother Dominic the monk praising the photocopier as otherworldly ("It's a miracle!"). Today, IBM ads show nuns and anthropologists and—yes—more monks worshiping laptops. Television commercials trumpet the virtues of the information superhighway. The unambiguous message is, *this technology will bring us all closer together; it will establish peace and harmony; it will improve life in every way imaginable.*

In reality, technology will not lead to nirvana. But grand expectations continue because of the wonder and awe inspired by each new technology. I know about these expectations, these false hopes, because like virtually everyone in my generation, I'm infected with them.

When I was in college, I got my first Macintosh—*exhilaration.* As a young reporter, I got my first Powerbook laptop. Now I'm really free, I thought, because I can take my work anywhere.

But, of course, I was also hooked. I became so dependent on my laptop, the thought of life without it became utterly terrifying. Yet another Apple product had become deeply ingrained in my identity. As much as any phrase that I can think of to accurately describe who I am, I am a Mac-person.

It took me years to make my first pilgrimage to Apple headquarters in the city of Cupertino, forty minutes south of San Francisco. But when I finally did, I wasn't disappointed. In fact, I felt like wide-eyed Charlie on his first glimpse of Willy Wonka's chocolate factory. As I steered my car onto the Saratoga/Sunnyvale exit ramp off Highway 280 and got a sudden and unexpected glimpse of the large, beaming, rainbow-colored apple, my heart broke into a gallop. And as Apple's off-white cubist complex of buildings came into view, my thoughts drifted back to my first Macintosh computer, the very first model, in my freshman year in college (1984), when writing words and editing paragraphs were transformed from chores into ticklish adventures. This was the time when writing became almost as much fun as reading.

I turned onto Apple's private drive, "Infinite Loop," drove past a garden of vividly colored life-size Macintosh icons—a giant hand, a giant dog, a giant watch (all bordered by jagged edges so as to resemble the icons on a pixelated screen), and pulled into the head-quarters of Apple Computer, Inc., indisputably my favorite corporation on Earth. For me, and for many others, the machine known as the Macintosh has been more than a handy word processor and fancy calculator; it has been a force of good, giving us an electronic palette with which we could, more easily than ever before, organize and clarify our thoughts—and rearrange them to come up with entirely new ideas. From the very start, the Mac was so easy and intuitive; it was like an add-on external brain, into which we could pour information, propositions, and critiques, and juxtapose them against one another in any fashion we could think up. A notepad simply records static thoughts; the Mac fluidly assists in the process of contemplation.

Plus, it was a jazz to play with. Personal computers help to turn life into a daily game—the adrenaline buzz from constantly improving efficiency of thought and information transfer, the constant upgrades and the feeling that by taming a thinking machine, you are rising above your ordinary mortal self, pushing the envelope of what humanity is capable of. To operate such a reliable, intuitive computer is to every day feel a sliver of what an Edison or a Wright or an Oppenheimer felt: to rise above the earthly coil of man, to defy nature, to fly, to have light all night long, to have machines think for us. "The IBM is a machine you can respect," remarked Lotus software pioneer Mitch Kapor just as the Mac was being rolled out. "The Macintosh is a machine you can love."

As a matter of fact, this kind of devotion was the explicit goal of Jef Raskin, the person who named and first conceptualized the Mac. "The purpose of this design," he wrote in 1980 in his collection of notes he called *The Book of Macintosh*, "is to create a low-cost portable computer so useful that its owner misses it when it's not around . . . a nearly indispensable companion." *Mission accomplished,* millions of longtime Mac users can testify, including me. Since that first Macintosh a dozen years ago, I have rarely been away from mine. There is no other object or person I have spent as much time with.

Millions could make the exact same admission. With the introduction of the Mac and its imitators in the mid-'80s, an army of young adults started to spend a lot more time at their desks. So as I parked my car in the Apple parking lot and made my way up the walkway to greet an old schoolmate working there, there was a certain amount of reverence in my smile. This was more than a company to me. It was an indelible part of my creative identity. That giant apple icon spoke to me in emotional tones. It said, "Further."

But this was, after all, still a corporation. A receptionist greeted and registered me (on a Mac, of course, which spat out a name tag). In a few minutes, my friend Dean appeared with the sagging eyes of an overworked programmer and a friendly, relaxed hello, and walked me into the four-story domed atrium. Dean had been at Apple for five years, ever since he graduated from college. He was now a senior research scientist with Apple's Advanced Technology Group. After a quick tour through the AT Lab (it was everything one would imagine it should be—a glorified playpen with a series of soft leather couches, jumbo-screen televisions, a giant idea board, and so on), we came to his small, well-lighted office, which had four or five computers (all for him), video cameras, microphones, and a few hundred feet of cable tying everything together and linking him with the rest of the company and—via the Internet—the planet. Another fantasy land, for any computer buff. Dean was designing QuickTime Conferencing, a state-of-the-art software tool that would soon enable any two or more computer users to collaborate in real time over their computers using text, audio, and video.

I told him how I'd gotten a little choked up when I first pulled up and saw the Apple campus. He nodded. "I felt exactly the same way when I first got here," he said. There was a pause. "I'm a little bit more cynical now."

It turned out, very much to my surprise, that my old friend who was deep in the belly of the information revolution was very open to my newly ambivalent feelings about technology's unintended consequences. As I started to rattle off some of my concerns, he recalled a recent incident. He had just taken his car in for service and, among other things, had asked the mechanic to rotate the tires. Then he watched helplessly as the mechanic struggled to spell "rotate." "He got to r-o-t and finally gave up," Dean said. Dean wanted to help him, but feared it would be condescending and inappropriate. As our advanced technologist came face-to-face with the other America, he had no choice but to pretend to be distracted, to not notice what was going on.

"This guy is illiterate," Dean said. "I'm sitting there thinking, 'How on earth is the information revolution—or whatever you want to call it—going to help him?'"

Apple Computer was started in 1976 by Steve Jobs and Steve Wozniak with the express purpose of building a computer for the "common man." But as Dean the Quicktime designer came face-to-face with the illiterate mechanic, it couldn't have been more clear to him that the Apple mission was far from successful. "Steve Jobs set out to make a computer that would empower all people," Dean told me. "But that hasn't happened yet." Perhaps the leading enthusiast of the personal computing age, Jobs too was apparently seduced by *techne,* believing that his new, powerful, intuitive machines could be socially progressive beyond all expectations. As a demonstration of his faith, he early on announced a plan to give away an Apple computer to every school in the nation. In 1983 he lured Pepsi president John Sculley to the top job at Apple with the self-righteous dare: "Do you want to sell sugar water for the rest of your life, or do you want to come with me and change the world?"

As early renditions of the personal computer made their way into the world, the old techno-utopian fever was revived yet again.

Interest led to excitement, which led to overexcitement and false hope that this wasn't just an exciting new appliance. It was going to change the world—*save* the world. "A revolution is under way that will change forever the way an entire nation works, plays, travels, and even thinks," *Newsweek* declared in 1980. "Just as the industrial revolution dramatically expanded the strength of man's muscles and the reach of his hand, so the smart-machine revolution will *magnify the power of his brain.*"

Another decade, another technology, same utopian fever: The Internet has inspired not only many thoughtful appraisals but also the bluster of blushing information Pollyannas who believe it can do no wrong. "Within a few years," projected the *New York Post* in 1993, "consumers across the country will, at the flick of a switch, have access to an almost infinite amount of information. . . . All except Luddites and hole-in-the-wall reactionaries will rejoice at this potential expansion of human capabilities."

An infinite amount of information. Imagine that. It is as if information is a renewable fuel, and all we need to do is simply plug our computers and our brain stems into the global network in order to be supplied with everything we need to live happy, healthy, wealthy lives.

What kind of techno-sap would fall for such a preposterous notion?

Me, for one. In 1991, in the midst of my obsession with the Mac, I fell just as hard for the joys of the Internet. It instantly multiplied the importance of the computer in my life. In addition to being the focal point of my thought and creativity, it was now also an unprecedented tool for communication. I joined an electronic bulletin board called the WELL, short for Whole Earth 'Lectronic Link, also based in the Bay Area. My first e-mail address was the labyrinthine well!dshenk@lll-winken.llnl.gov. I sent e-mail to friends in Israel and Oregon and was thrilled to get replies back within a day or so. Here is a record of my zeal, an excerpt from one of my earliest electronic letters to a few friends:

3/3/91

. . . This e-mail apparatus, and the further possibility of a real ongoing electronic conference, is the first thing I have come upon that provides us with a viable opportunity to Have It All, nearly, in terms of our communication wants . . . it is potentially a real ongoing consciousness between all of us, as opposed to the choppy set up (at best) that we have now—e.g. "did you ever get that letter that I wrote six weeks ago?" . . .

I wonder who else has e-mail potential? Beth? Wilkins? Rog? Erez? Sharone? There are hundreds of great minds out there who [sic] we are already familiar with, who could be a valuable part of an ongoing discussion of lifestuffs. This is as much about how we're going to communicate over the next 50 years as it is about the next 50 days. . . .

A few weeks later, one friend in Israel sent me a reply via ordinary postal "snail" mail. "Dave: you are obsessed by e-mail. Have you sought professional counseling?"

Looking back now, I can certainly see his point. I was under a spell, dreaming the techno-utopian dream in the great tradition of Sarnoff, Bush, and Gates. That's what these machines can do to a person, or even a whole society. To those of us who are a little disappointed with the present, they serve as a convenient totem on which to pin our hopes for a quick, easy solution to our troubles. *Here's a fantastical new machine to get us out of this jam . . .*

The tradition continues in full splendor with the contemporary mania to connect all American classrooms to the Internet by the year 2000. Bill Clinton has fallen into the techno-utopian trap, and is dragging the rest of us along with him. "We can revolutionize education" by connecting schools to the Internet, Clinton promises. Reed Hundt, Clinton's FCC chairman, has posed our schools' crisis in this way: "There are thousands of buildings in this country with millions of people in them who have no telephones, no cable television and no reasonable prospect of broadband services. They're called schools." Without any serious discussion at all, the devotion in Washington to computer-boosted education has already led to a major national push to wire all the schools in the country by the year 2000.

This fixation with computers in the classroom is understandable. Relatively speaking, it is a cheap and quick fix. The problem is, it's not a fix at all. To those who don't have a vested interest in coming up with an instant solution to our education challenges or selling a lot of computer equipment, computers in the classroom do not look like such a terrific idea. "Perhaps the saddest occasion for me is to be taken to a computerized classroom and be shown children joyfully using computers," Alan Kay, one of the legendary pioneers of personal computing, testified to Congress in 1995. "They are happy, the teachers and administrators are happy, and their parents are happy. Yet, in most such classrooms, on closer examination I can see that the children are doing nothing interesting or growth-inducing at all! This is technology as a kind of junk food—people love it but there is no nutrition to speak of. At its worst, it is a kind of 'cargo cult' in which it is thought that the mere presence of computers will somehow bring learning back to the classroom."

The unspoken assumption behind such an effort is that computers and telephones and cable television are vital educational tools. This is based on wishful thinking, not analysis or common sense. "I used to think that technology could help education," Steve Jobs said in 1996. "I've probably spearheaded giving away more computer equipment to schools than anybody else on the planet. But I've had to come to the inevitable conclusion that the problem is not one that technology can hope to solve. . . . You're not going to solve the problems by putting all knowledge onto CD-ROMs . . . Lincoln did not have a Website at the log cabin where his parents home-schooled him, and he turned out pretty interesting. Historical precedent shows that we can turn out amazing human beings without technology. Precedent also shows that we can turn out very uninteresting human beings with technology."

These protests reveal not only a welcome clearing of the techno-utopian haze, but also an insight into the misunderstanding behind the idea of computers as educational tools. The process of creating intelligence is not merely a question of access to information. Would that learning were as easy as diving into a swimming pool of information or sitting down at a great banquet table for an info-feast. Rather, education, which comes from the Latin *educare*, meaning to raise and nurture, is more a matter of imparting values and critical faculties than inputting raw data. Education is about enlightenment, not just access.

In fact, the earliest schools in America were founded not to instill knowledge per se, but to instill religious social values. "If any children in the neighborhood are under no education," Cotton Mather wrote, "don't allow 'em to continue so. Let care be taken that they may be better educated, and taught to read, and be taught their catechism and the truths and ways of their only savior." Even today, all schools have underlying value systems. Most are not explicitly religious, but are still run according to specific values such as the importance of personal liberty and private property. Schools exist for a social purpose; packing as much information as possible into each classroom hardly serves that purpose. Education cannot be fixed with a digital pipeline of data.

The Fourth Law of Data Smog
Putting a computer in every classroom is like putting an electric power plant in every home.

Schools are stringent filters, not expansive windows onto the world. Teachers and textbooks block out the vast majority of the world's information, allowing into the classroom only very small bits of information at any given time. When organized well and cogently presented, these parcels of data are metamorphosized into building blocks of knowledge in the brains of students.

The computer, by and large, is designed for a very different purpose. It helps access and deliver enormous stores of information at high speeds. It is not a filter, but a pump. As a library-type resource, it can be a terrific value. But it is not, as some have argued, an inherently superior classroom tool. This is not to deny the efficacy of certain thoughtful and highly disciplined educational software programs. But to leap from the reasonable claim that *computers can be a useful tool in education* to an insistence that powerful high-speed computers are destined to revolutionize classroom education simply on the basis of their power and speed is to let the winds of techno-utopianism sweep us away.

If the dichotomy between past expectations and today's reality is any guide, we certainly cannot expect information technology to deliver us to a new generation of geniuses. Rather we'll have to create our genius the old-fashioned way. We'll have to *learn* it.

PART 2

Virtual Anarchy

We are, all of us, being drawn into the
electronic world, and we can't stop it.
It's like being given a car without
anyone telling you how to drive it,
and you don't have a road map.
We're driving blind.

—Sandy Sparks, Lawrence
Livermore Laboratories

chapter 5

The Thunderbird Problem

And other "upgrade" pitfalls

There's an old episode of *Gilligan's Island*, I seem to recall, wherein our hapless castaways come upon a boat to take them back to civilization. But when they overload their rescue craft with unnecessary baggage (topped off with Thurston Howell III's trunk o' wealth), it sinks about twenty seconds after they cast off. After a frantic swim in the lagoon, it is back to the tropic island mist for Skipper, Little Buddy, and the gang.

Whether one is packing a suitcase or making a sundae at a self-serve ice cream bar, the temptation to keep piling on is often irresistible, and is invariably followed by feelings of deep regret. When it comes to information technology, though, add-ons are a special problem, with especially vexing consequences.

Adam, a friend from high school, became an expert in computer-assisted journalism and wound up with a job at Microsoft. I flew out to Seattle to visit him for a few days. He took me into his office one morning—yes, we stopped at Starbucks on the way—to introduce me to some of Microsoft's programming luminaries. At the end of the day, I put down my reporter's notebook and shifted back into consumer mode as Adam took me on a swing through the Microsoft store, where employees are able to buy software for 80 percent off.

Eighty percent! The fantasy shopping spree lives in Redmond, Washington. My eyes darted around the store maniacally and my pulse raced as I snatched stacks of CD-ROMs and software upgrades from each aisle. I could see no logical stopping point, so I relied on the limits of Adam's patience. Among other items, I bought myself Microsoft Word 6.0, yet another upgrade of the program I had been using for ten years or so (I began with 1.0, and over the years have upgraded to 2.something, 3.1, then 4.0, and 5.0, 5.1, and now 6). With Adam's discount ("Adam" is not his real name), Word 6.0 cost me just $10. It seemed like a terrific bargain for dozens of sensational new formatting features like AutoCorrect, AutoText, 100-level Undo, drag-and-drop editing, Table AutoFormat, and something called "Wizards."

But it turned out to be wasted cash. After I took the time to install all thirteen high-density disks onto my hard drive (the previous upgrade had been just six disks), I found Word 6.0 to be painfully slow and cumbersome. The upgrade was advertised as having a "built-in intelligence that senses what you want to do and produces the desired result, making routine tasks automatic and complex jobs easier." But all the new bells and whistles had transformed the program I depended on for basic word processing into a veritable zoo of capabilities that were cumbersome to learn, and had slowed down even the most elemental functions, like opening a file and printing, to a painful crawl. This minor fiasco raised the obvious question in my mind: If it wasn't broke, why had they tried so hard to fix it?

The answer, I discovered, is that upgrades are the lifeblood of the information industry. Understanding the ramifications of this fact is critical to a complete comprehension of the new social dynamics of the information society.

When I later visited K., I told him about my disappointment with Word 6.0. He nodded in recognition. "Oh, yes," he said, "you're talking about the Thunderbird Problem."

The Thunderbird Problem is an industry term for the dark side of the upgrade phenomenon, named after the excruciating transformation of the legendary Ford Thunderbird over the last several decades. When first introduced in the mid-1950s, the T-bird was a sleek, adventurous, charming automobile. But the nature of the American automobile business was such that no design was allowed to last. Instead, cars were changed significantly enough each year so that customers would feel compelled to "trade-up" to feel *current*.

This strategy of "planned obsolescence" focused not on real improvement, but on the superficial appearance of progress. Quality was sacrificed to the sales imperative. Bit by bit, with no one looking out for the integrity of the vehicle itself, the original charm and grace of many cars were stripped away. The T-bird is by no means an aberration; it just happens to be one of the best illustrations of the problem.

1950s Thunderbird

1990s Thunderbird

And so it is with software and hardware, K. explained. A product starts out reasonably simple and smart, but in the effort to convince consumers to upgrade, a long string of bells and whistles are added on year after year, to the point where both the aesthetics and performance of the original product are often diluted.

Dean, my friend at Apple, was also immediately familiar with the notion when I visited him in his office. "That's exactly what happened to the Macintosh," he said. Each year, Apple had expanded the capabilities of the machine to the point where, in Dean's opinion, it had lost its essence. One obvious example of this was that the latest generation of Powerbooks, which were supposed to be many times more powerful and speedy than my two-year-old machine, came so loaded down with software that they were actually much slower.

The Thunderbird Problem is endemic to the era of superabundance. We upgrade because we so easily can. In our enthusiasm for the next magical phase, we lose sight of the original purpose. We add and add and add until one day we find that we've got a trunk full of useless trinkets onboard and the ship is taking on water.

Mostly, this beastly situation continues because it's terrifically profitable. Planned computer obsolescence reaps billions of dollars every year for programmers, manufacturers, marketers, and public relations professionals. Consumers do not, after all, ever have the benefit of the following experience:

[PLACE: ACME MICROCOMPUTERS OUTLET]

JOE SALESGUY: Beauty, ain't she?

JEREMY CONSUMER: What are the specs on this machine?

JOE: One hundred and fifty megahertz. One-gigabyte hard drive. Built-in 28.8 fax modem and four-speed CD-ROM. With the rebate, you can take it home today for $1,800.

JEREMY: That sounds reasonable. I'll take it.

JOE: Great, they'll ring you up at the desk, you can pick up your machine at the counter on the right, and we'll see you again in about eighteen months.

JEREMY: Excuse me?

JOE: Oh sure, you'll be back before you know it to get a much faster machine with more storage for about the same money. This baby will still work like a charm, but it'll feel real sluggish compared to the new ones coming into your office. Colleagues will point at yours and call it a dinosaur. Then one day you'll hear about the latest version of your favorite software, and you'll see the asterisk noting that it won't work on your machine without a lot more RAM. Meanwhile, the twenty-speed CD-ROM drives will be coming out, making your four-speed seem pretty pathetic . . .

No clerk will ever acknowledge such an *unrefined* truth in a real sales pitch, of course. But every day, as people purchase software and hardware, speedy obsolescence is *the* subtext. Remember Windows 95? As Microsoft introduced its much-anticipated system upgrade, they were able to generate so much interest (with the help of Jay Leno and the Rolling Stones) that some computer stores opened up at midnight to sell the first copies, just as music stores occasionally do for big pop records.

But how hot was Windows 95 in 1996? If it felt like old news, that's because Microsoft had planned it that way. Sure enough, an upgrade—Windows 98—will roll out shortly after this book's publication. Since Microsoft, like all the others, makes most of its profits on upgrades, the real product isn't hardware or software, but *information anxiety.* In order to satisfy Wall Street's short-term outlook, the corporate challenge becomes convincing the consumer to pay for upgrades as often as possible.

The Fifth Law of Data Smog

What they sell is not information technology, but information anxiety.

The sales goal of the information industry is to convince consumers that, whatever they have, it isn't enough. It works. At the beginning of this decade, IBM found that people were replacing their computers every five years. By 1995 computer users were considering their machines obsolete in just *two* years. Judging by the current rate of return, it is estimated that by the year 2005, the nation will have tossed 150 million computers into the scrap bucket. So, while we pretend to buy a machine only for its technical capabilities, there is apparently a powerful hidden social component to each purchase: keeping up with the Joneses.

This is what's behind the inexplicable disdain for machines just a few years old. *I've got this 286 in my closet—it's a dinosaur.* What two years ago was a critical piece of machinery now seems like useless plastic. We act as though the machine has actually lost its technical abilities, when of course it is we, not the machine, who have changed. What else besides effective marketing and intense social pressure could sway our own perceptions so dramatically in such a short period of time?

Even though the machines themselves could last for years and years, computers are *socially perishable.* To really participate in the information revolution, one must abide by the tenets of Moore's Law—the industry's rule of thumb that computer processing speed doubles every two years or so—and one must "upgrade" machinery approximately that often. Which I have done, faithfully:

1. Apple II Plus (52K floppy drive, 48K RAM, 6502 processor), *1982*

2. Macintosh (400K floppy, 128K RAM, 68000 processor), *1984*

3. Mac512 (same, with 512K RAM), *1985*

4. Mac SE30 (800K floppy, 10 MB hard drive, 68030 processor), *1988*

5. Mac Classic (20MB hard drive, 1.4MB floppy, 2MB RAM, 68000 processor), *1989*

6. Powerbook 140 (40MB hard drive, 1.4MB floppy, 4MB RAM, 68030 processor), *1991*

7. Upgrade: 80 MB hard drive, *1992*

8. Powerbook 180 (same, with 120MB hard drive), *1993*

9. Upgrade: 340 MB hard drive, *1995*

I offer this list not as a boast but as a *mea culpa*. While personal computers have been relatively inexpensive compared to their costly, bulky predecessors in the 1960s and '70s, the pace of improvements is such that the personal computer *habit* has been anything but cheap. Computer junkies sometimes jokingly discuss the astronomic costs of their lifestyle by distinguishing "computer-dollars" from "real-dollars." "Did you ever notice how, for anything else, $300 is a lot of money?" a friend remarks as we drool over CD-ROM drives in a computer store. "But in the computer universe, we don't think twice about spending it." As with exotic sports cars and renowned paintings on the auction block, the price is not measured in rational terms. And while personal computers are touted for their cost-effectiveness, the cost of keeping up with the pace of change is extraordinarily expensive.

This social perishability of computer technology isn't merely a problem for computer enthusiasts like me. The momentum driving me to upgrade my hardware and software every few months is part of the same force pushing your health care premiums through the roof. As technology accelerates the pace of change for every industry dependent on it, it also extracts a seemingly constant stream of "upgrade" fees for new software and hardware, and for worker retraining. Not far from the Microsoft campus near Seattle is another software titan, Oracle Corporation. Oracle, the second largest software company, has profited handsomely from the sales of its database management and client/server software, and is now considered a top Internet player and one of the shrewdest scouts for future opportunities in our emerging information economy. In the summer of 1996, Oracle instituted a major shift in its business in order to take advantage of what it saw emerging as a potentially lucrative market of the future: technology-driven *inexperience.* "We see a training gap," said Oracle's Bill Seawick. "Technology is coming at such a fantastic pace that people have to learn new technologies every three or four months."

Millions of recently "downsized" Americans, rendered obsolete and jobless by technology, would not contest Seawick's assessment. Neither would U.S. Labor Secretary Robert Reich, who has made worker-retraining a personal crusade, warning that in today's economy everyone can expect to change jobs an average of seven or eight times in their lifetime. Job stability, Reich says, is a thing of the past.

There is also a social cost to upgrade mania that cannot be measured in dollars. The blistering pace of life today, driven by technology and the business imperative to improve efficiency, is something to behold. We often feel life going by much, much faster than we wish, as we are carried forward from meeting to meeting, call to call, errand to errand. We have less time to ourselves, and are expected to improve our performance and output year after year after year. If life were a cartoon, as it sometimes seems to be, we would be the breathless Wile E. Coyote, forever chasing the Road Runner but never concluding the chase *(<beep beep>).*

Upgrade training may be the growth industry of the future, but it won't heal all the scars from the ever-accelerating pace of change. There is a psychic consequence to this blistering pace. When Americans tell pollsters and therapists that they feel they are losing control over the basic structures of their lives, it's partly because they are. The ferocious upgrading of the machinery all around us undermines our sense of security and continuity.

Finally, upgrade mania also undermines our technical grasp of history. In the National Archives in College Park, Maryland (just outside Washington, D.C.), a massive amount of government data is being stockpiled in electronic form, but with great trepidation. Safely warehoused in temperature- and humidity-controlled rooms, the data will be intact for hundreds if not thousands of years to come. But will our children be able to access it? "You can get an optical disk that may last for a hundred years," says Archives Director of Electronic Storage Kenneth Thibodeau of the dilemma facing all modern archivists. "But in *ten* years you won't be able to find a drive to read the thing." The technology changes so quickly that librarians, archivists, and corporate systems managers will forever be playing catch-up, at enormous effort and expense.

It makes one wonder whether whatever we are all chasing is worth the chase itself.

Should you drink coffee? . . .
Hardly a month goes by without
the release of yet another study linking
coffee or caffeine to some undesirable
health effect or absolving it of a
suspected hazard. But almost
without fail, such reports are soon
followed by studies that fail to
confirm either the risks
or the benefits.

—Jane E. Brody,
The New York Times

chapter 6

Paralysis by Analysis

I t was a mild spring morning in Washington, D.C., in 1993, when the Supreme Court of the United States went head-to-head against the information glut, and was apparently bested. "I'm a little lost," conceded Justice Sandra Day O'Connor to her colleagues on the bench.

The case confounding Justice O'Connor stemmed from the physical distress of a little boy named Jason Daubert, whose severe birth defects, his parents alleged, could be blamed on the antinausea drug Bendectin. Jason's parents were suing Bendectin's manufacturer, Merrell Dow Pharmaceuticals, on the basis of a study linking the drug to birth defects in animals. But their case had twice been thrown out of court even before reaching a jury, because in the face of other contradictory research, the judges had ruled the animal study inadmissible. Without this crucial piece of evidence, there was simply no case.

On appeal, the Daubert case ultimately made it to the Supreme Court because it epitomized the growing conflict between our burgeoning culture of specialization and our legal system. Courts have long struggled with the issue of expert testimony, because of its inherent power of intimidation over layperson juries. How is a juror without any technical education to judge a microscopic fiber analysis or a complex medical evaluation?

For this reason, our court system is inherently antitechnical by design. It is also extremely restrictive of information. It is a fundamental legal tenet that justice is insured by the severe limitation of witnesses, exhibits, and testimony. In order to ensure a fair trial, juries are not allowed to come into contact with "hearsay" or any other information that doesn't pass strict legal tests of relevance. In this way, we arrive not necessarily at a final truth, but at as fair and just a ruling as time and circumstances allow.

For most of this century, expert testimony was restricted by the "Frye rule," a 1923 court decision prohibiting experts from introducing in court opinions not "generally accepted" in the scientific community. But in 1975 Congress gutted the Frye rule by allowing a wide range of so-called experts to testify on anything deemed relevant, including hearsay evidence. Following that change, courts were overrun with what critics called "junk science"—testimony not scientifically credible, but packaged well enough to persuade nonexpert judges and jurors. Thus the importance of *Daubert* v. *Merrell Dow*. Scientists were anticipating that this case would be one of the most important in the century.

To the justices, however, it was more immediately a tangled mess of scientific mumbo jumbo. In the oral arguments, they were forced to wallow in the very muck from which they were seeking to protect juries. As Charles Fried, the attorney representing Merrell Dow, argued that the animal research was not relevant to the Daubert case, the nonscientist justices quickly found themselves as helpless as a night driver with no headlights. "How are we supposed to know this, Mr. Fried?" Chief Justice William Rehnquist interrupted him in frustration. "You're a lawyer, not a doctor. You may know, but I don't."

Without realizing it, Rehnquist was speaking on behalf of ordinary citizens everywhere. So was Justice Harry Blackmun, when he issued this desperate plea to both sides: "There are Harvard science professors all over this case. Couldn't you get them together, and lead us out of the wilderness?"

The Sixth Law of Data Smog
Too many experts spoil the clarity.

The proliferation of expert opinion has ushered in a virtual anarchy of expertise. To follow the news today is to have the surreal understanding that the earth is melting *and* the earth is cooling; that nuclear power is safe and nuclear power is *not* safe; that affirmative action works—or wait, *no it doesn't.* In the era of limitless data, there is always an opportunity to crunch some more numbers, spin them a bit, and prove the opposite. Would jobs have been gained or lost under Bill Clinton's comprehensive health care plan? Is dioxin as dangerous as we once thought? Do vitamins prevent cancer? With the widening pool of elaborate studies and arguments on every side of every question, more expert knowledge has, paradoxically, led to less clarity.

The New York Times aptly calls this phenomenon "volleys of data." Statistics and hard facts are one of the fundamental ingredients of a just and civil society; but as with other forms of information, it turns out that too much of a good thing can have unwelcome consequences. The dramatic reduction in the cost of information production and distribution has ushered in an era of seemingly endless argumentation. "Much of the Congressional battle about President Clinton's economic package could come down to a duel over algebra," wrote the *Times'* Steven Greenhouse in 1993. "Republican mathematicians attack the President's plan as a tax-and-spend scheme, asserting that it includes $1.75 to $18 in tax increases for every dollar in spending cuts. Mr. Clinton's number crunchers respond that it is a prudent, balanced plan, with one dollar in revenue tax increases for each dollar in spending cuts. Which is right in this battle of the calculators? The answer, in the never-never land of American politics, is that both sides are, depending on how one cuts the deck."

Journalists and news consumers alike are stymied by the modern tendency of statistics to argue in every direction. Anyone who has attempted to conscientiously research a medical or political issue has confronted this problem directly: The endless analysis is so overwhelming, it is difficult to know how and when to decide.

Cyberspace enthusiasts have a favorite motto that they commonly employ in debates against people who favor regulation and censorship: *Information wants to be free.* By this they simply mean that digital information is so easily replicated and disseminated that the information itself takes on a libertarian personality (we'll elaborate on this in Part 3). But that freedom isn't completely without its drawbacks. As early as 1938, H. G. Wells recognized that the proliferation of information was feeding a cycle of perpetual intellectual conflict. For a technical problem, Wells proposed a technical solution—the aforementioned "World Brain," an electronic encyclopedia that, he argued, would "bring together into close juxtaposition and under critical scrutiny many apparently conflicting systems of statement [acting as a] clearing house of misunderstandings."

Alas, Wells's hopeful vision has not been realized. Instead, technology inadvertently adds to the confusion by generating more and more material and by making much of it instantly accessible.

On National Public Radio's *All Things Considered* one evening, reporter Chitra Ragavan is trying to make sense of the latest cancer study, which doesn't comport with previous studies. "If you don't have some level of confusion about how to interpret this study," the National Cancer Institute's Philip Taylor tells Ragavan, "you should."

Inconclusive results, Ragavan reports. More studies needed. "Other large studies now underway may help clear the confusion," she suggests hopefully. But in her optimism, she is ignoring source of contention. It is our tools that have gotten us i mess in the first place. With a majority of American workers i. paid to churn out data, we have generated a morass of expert information that has started to undermine logical approaches to deliberation and problem solving. Responding to a report that there have been more than 100,000 studies conducted on depression, the University of Chicago's Larry V. Hedges pleads: "Is this a sensible situation? Do we really need more data?"

The studies pour in at such a rate, in fact, that a new field of statistics—"meta-analysis"—has suddenly emerged to make sense of the glut. Meta-analysis, the study of studies, is a method of combining pools of statistics from a wide range of studies and making a comprehensive analysis based on the whole. Data from hundreds of different examinations into whether caffeine causes breast cancer will be pooled together into one giant study. Though the approach dates back to 1904, when English statistician Karl Pearson used data from a range of vaccinations to conclude that they were ineffective, meta-analysis was all but forgotten until the 1980s, when frustrated researchers began to turn to it as a way out of their statistical confusion. By 1992 meta-analysis was so common it was formally endorsed by the National Research Council.

Does it work? We may never know. The modern confusion created by the glut of statistics also plagues this would-be solution. Meta-analysis, sums up the journal *Science,* is a "controversial method that has provoked dispute in every field to which it has been applied. . . . [despite this,] proponents of the method argue that whatever problems there are in the technique will have to be dealt with, because there is no other way to handle the explosion of data."

The statistical anarchy freezes us in our cerebral tracks. The psychological reaction to such an overabundance of information and competing expert opinions is to simply avoid coming to conclusions. "You can't choose any one study, any one voice, any one spokesperson for a point of view," explains psychologist Robert Cialdini. "So what do you do? It turns out that the answer is: you don't do anything. *You reserve judgment.* You wait and see what the predominance of opinion evolves to be."

"But," Cialdini continues, confronting the paradox, "I don't know that we have the luxury to wait that long, in modern life."

As the amount of information and competing claims stretches toward infinity, the concern is that we may be on the verge of a whole new wave of indecisiveness: paralysis by analysis. (In this way, technology brings with it yet another internal contradiction: As it speeds up our world in the name of efficiency and productivity, it also constricts rational thinking.)

With a seemingly endless thirst for facts and figures, and a nagging ambivalence and indecisiveness plaguing his decision-making style, Bill Clinton is information morass incarnate, the eery embodiment of Cialdini's warning. To listen to him speak extemporaneously about an issue is to witness a man able to grasp so much data, he frequently becomes engulfed in it. This was much in evidence immediately after the 1992 presidential election, in a lengthy post-campaign, pre-inaugural economic summit, where the President-elect appeared to be more of an economics professor—bathing in data for data's sake—than a leader trying to settle on policies to achieve his goals. Unfortunately, reports indicate that he also exhibited these same traits in the White House. "Clinton carried a lot of information in his head," writes journalist Elizabeth Drew, "something that didn't always work to his advantage. Reagan, being underinformed, could be utterly clear about his simple goals; Clinton, being *exceedingly informed,* sometimes got lost in his facts." (This is not to say that Reagan's childlike simplicity is desirable; one does not want a president to be factually malnourished.)

White House staffers complained to Drew that Clinton was too bogged down in details, that he was fond of delivering "an intense seminar on government minutiae." "One of the reasons for the indecisiveness demonstrated in [White House] meetings," writes Drew, "was that, 'Clinton never stops thinking.' Another [White

House staffer] said, 'There were a lot of last-minute decisions and changes. That's Clinton's way.'" Afflicted with a particularly acute case of what political scientist Ross Baker calls "dataholism," Clinton is not an exception but a mere exaggeration.

Civilization has thrived on an increasing diet of science and other reliable statistics. Applied data has answered millions of important questions about how to live a better life. But with today's runaway pace of information, we may have come upon too much of a good thing. Information may want to be free, but that freedom in and of itself isn't enough to support humanity. We also depend on information's integrity, and not a little discipline.

chapter 7

Stat Wars

Since nearly any argument imaginable can now be supported with an impressive data set, the big winner is . . . argumentation itself. Journalist Michael Kinsley calls this "stat wars." Factionalism gets a big boost from the volleys of data, while dialogue and consensus—the marrow of democracy—run thinner and thinner every year. "Facts can have the same stupefying effect as images of flag factories and furloughed felons," writes Daniel Pink. As a 1992 campaign strategist for Senator Bob Kerrey, Pink used a computer to toy with the numbers in Bill Clinton's economic proposals in order to speciously argue that Clinton planned to cut $7.5 billion from Social Security. "Facts," Pink says from experience, "can manipulate and mislead."

Nowhere are the stat wars more heated than in Washington, D.C.

From CNN's *Crossfire:*

PAT BUCHANAN, co-host: Arkansas was fourth highest in teen pregnancy when [Dr. Joycelyn Elders] took over. Now, it's second or first. Under her program of condom distribution and the rest, STDs, sexually transmitted diseases, the incidence of them have soared. . . .

DR. WALTER FAGGETT, National Medical Association: You take it out of context, Pat. That's the problem. Again, the teenage pregnancy rate in Arkansas—the rate of increase has decreased.

MICHAEL KINSLEY, co-host: And the rate of increase in Arkansas is lower than the rate of increase in the rest of the country.

RALPH REED, The Christian Coalition: No, it isn't. Between 1987 and 1992, teen pregnancy increased in Arkansas by 15 percent, at the time that it was increasing at 5 percent at the national average. It's gotten a lot worse.

MICHAEL KINSLEY: The statistic I saw was 17 percent in Arkansas, but it was 18 percent in the country.

In our nation's capital, supplying grist for endless policy debates has become a vital industry over the last several decades. Public relations agencies profit handsomely for fanning debates, and television shows like *Crossfire* are specifically designed to exploit the entertainment value of the stat wars phenomenon. The charges come flying back and forth across the table as furiously as a Ping-Pong ball. But there is no referee and no official scoring; the show always ends before viewers have time to gauge the accuracy of the shots. Stay tuned for tomorrow night, when a new volley of stats will be on view—supplied at no charge by D.C.'s stat war munitions factories. To stock up on data, lobbyists and *Crossfire* producers need only flip through a local phone book:

With purposefully vague and formidable names like Institute for Responsive Government and the National Center for Policy Analysis, hundreds of so-called think tanks have popped up in our nation's capital since the late 1960s. Staffed with some of the most skilled polemicists and statisticians in the land and generously supported by American corporations with specific political agendas, their task is to produce mountains of data to support partisan policy objectives. In the stat war environment, bulk is often as critical as quality. "In the Washington swirl, where few people have the time actually to read the reports they debate," explains Gregg Easterbrook in a definitive report on the think tank culture for *The Atlantic Monthly,* "respectability is often proportional to tonnage. The more studies someone tosses on the table, the more likely he is to win his point." These institutions are masters of contention. A good many of them are expressly uninterested in an earnest pursuit of the truth. "We're not here to be some kind of Ph.D. committee giving equal time," says Burton Pines, a leader of the right-wing Heritage Foundation. "Our role is to provide conservative public-policy makers with arguments to bolster our side. We're not troubled over this. There are plenty of think tanks on the other side."

As a matter of fact, though, since the late 1970s, the think-tank field has been heavily dominated by corporate money and conservative political philosophy. With dozens of corporatist, "free-enterprise" institutions (Cato, Manhattan, and Hudson institutes; the Reason Foundation; the Ethics and Public Policy Center, and so on) pushing for lower taxes and less regulation, "conservative commentators have their liberal counterparts outgunned by a wide margin," writes Easterbrook.

The American Enterprise Institute (AEI) is one of the oldest and most influential think tanks in town. Established as a pro-business mouthpiece in 1943 by industrialist Lewis Brown, it caught the conservative tide in the early '80s, more than tripling in size. A substantial portion of its multimillion-dollar budget comes from defense contractors, pharmaceutical companies, and banks. The Institute's mission, explains Vincent Sollitto, AEI's director of media relations, "is to do substantive research on public policy issues, to make sure that Congress is aware of all the possible options . . . especially the ones that reflect our own personal core beliefs—free market, limited government, free and fair trade, competitive enterprise, personal property rights, individual responsibility, and a strong and vibrant national defense."

Shaping the mood of Washington begins with expert press play, and every think tank has a point person to coordinate the constant flow. "I probably have 4,000 to 5,000 journalists on my system," estimates Sollitto. "That's just about every journalist in the world. They are cross-referenced in a tier form—national media, regional media, trade press, foreign press, and then cross-referenced by interest code—people interested in the environment, in economics, in other topics." With an incessant stream of articles, books, surveys, statistical analyses, AEI's forty-five scholars are constantly churning out material. "Everyone is expected to produce," Sollitto explains. "There isn't a policy issue that we're not somehow working on."

Think tanks aren't the only institutions to have become information hyper-producers. As information technology has made research, word processing, and publishing all dramatically cheaper, tens of millions of us have become our own think tanks—putting our ideas onto paper and/or disk and seeking an audience for our thoughts and opinions. Web home pages and neighborhood 'zines have turned millions of citizens into *glutizens*—reporters, publishers and broadcasters. The media is us. We aren't just splashing around in the information glut. We're also creating it.

chapter 8

The Two-by-Four Effect

Information glut and the coarsening of culture

Back in the seventh grade, in my hometown of Wyoming, Ohio, the most effective technique we could come up with for getting fellow students to read a flyer about an upcoming bake sale or student council meeting was to lead off with the words, "SEX SEX SEX: Now that we've gotten your attention . . . "

This old crudity came to mind recently after I received an e-mail from a stranger with the provocative subject heading, "I Found Your ATM Card." I was not aware that I had *lost* my ATM card, but of course I quickly passed up other unread e-mail to find out what was up.

Now that I've got your attention . . .

The e-mail had nothing to do with ATM cards after all. "I Found Your ATM Card" was just a glut-conscious ploy by someone who suspected, correctly, that I regularly receive a lot of e-mail, and who wanted to ensure that I would pay close attention to his. To break through the cloud of data smog surrounding me, he resorted to the tactic of shock.

Now imagine millions of people resorting to tactics like this every day. One of the most vivid consequences of the information glut is a culture awash in histrionics. People have discovered that, in order to get their messages across, they increasingly must wrap them in provocative or titillating packages. As the competition heats up, we do what we have to do to make our voices heard. We TALK LOUDER. Wear more color. Show more cleavage. Say shocking things.

In the immediate sense, pumping up the volume is an extremely effective solution. More broadly, though, it becomes part of the problem, feeding a vicious spiral in which the data smog gets thicker and thicker and the efforts to cut through the smog get ever more desperate. As the people of earth collectively try to rise above the noise, they unwittingly create more of it. The volume and vulgarity increase notch by notch, alongside the glut.

The Seventh Law of Data Smog
All high-stim roads lead to Times Square.

In a glutted environment, the most difficult task is not getting one's message out, but finding a receptive audience. As Stanley Milgram explained in 1970, individuals adapt to stimulus overload by allocating less time to each input, blocking reception whenever possible, and installing filtering devices to keep the number of inputs down to a manageable level. Metaphorically speaking, we plug up our ears, pinch our noses, cover our eyes with dark sunglasses, and step into a body suit lined with protective padding.

But this is not the end of the story. Inevitably, someone wishes to attract the attention of our overloaded, well-protected subject. Intuitively, the communicator responds to these new barriers with barrier-piercing countermeasures. In order to make contact with the person wearing earplugs, he raises his voice. To catch the eye of the person with sunglasses, he uses brighter lights. To make an impression on someone wearing a lot of protective padding, he gives that person a whack on the head. The predicament has become so common that there's already a popular American expression for it: "I had to hit him in the head with a two-by-four to get his attention."

And so it is that our glutted society is victimized by what we might call the "two-by-four effect." The two-by-four effect provides humanity with a way to keep communication alive in a glutted environment. But in so doing, it extracts a hefty price: Society, as we all know from experience, is becoming inexorably more crass. We are witnessing the new reign of trash TV, hate radio, shock jocks, tort litigation, publicity stunts, excessively violent and sarcastic rhetoric. Films are ever more sexually explicit and violent. Advertising is noisier, more invasive, and frequently skirting the bounds of taste ("What would you like on your tombstone," a firing squad chief asks a man he is about to execute. "Pepperoni," answers the blindfolded executee. It is an ad for Tombstone Pizza). Profanity is up, and common decency is down. A family-hour CBS sitcom character brags that, in order to keep the romance in his marriage, he "grabs her ass!" Such lines are not driven by loose morals, as crusader Bill Bennett has charged, but by the desire to capture an audience in a glutted media market. What Bennett has decried as "the coarsening of the culture" and what others have called our "crisis in family values" has more to do with the information revolution than it does with Hollywood's lack of respect for the traditional family model.

While we will have to wait to see how the technical aspects of the information revolution play themselves out, the basic character of our future information society has already been formed. Its colors are lighted in a blaze of neon; its audio track is full of expletives, insults, and explosions; and its cultural trademark is the ever-more-outrageous public relations stunt, such as the San Francisco radio station that offered a case of Snapple to the family of the one-thousandth person to commit suicide by jumping from the Golden

Gate Bridge. Radio shock jocks Don Imus and Howard Stern, who have over the last decade merchandised their gutter mouths into positions of national prominence and million-dollar salaries, are two of the chief beneficiaries of the two-by-four effect. Louis Farrakhan, spiritual leader to a tiny percentage of African-Americans, is another. Farrakhan has brilliantly parlayed his viciously anti-Semitic remarks into national media attention. Merely through controversy, he has attained a powerful stature.

The same can be said of Camille Paglia, Dennis Rodman, Madonna, Al Sharpton, Roseanne, Rush Limbaugh, Jesse Helms, Robert Dornan, Steven Bochco—the list of sensationalist attention-grubbers is virtually endless, because it is what many of our best and brightest now do for a living. Historically, discourteousness and vulgarity have always signified a lack of sophistication; garishness was considered tasteless and degrading. In today's attention-deficit society, however, people have learned that churlish behavior is the key to headlines, profit, and power. Thanks to the antics of these and many more talented sensationalists, our society is experiencing what communications scholar Kathleen Hall Jamieson calls "the normalization of hyperbole." Mouths become megaphones and advertisements become eye-popping, gut-wrenching dramas. Extreme measures to grab attention are not only condoned; they're admired. Outrageous behavior by individuals is rewarded with wealth and influence.

Not to mention *votes*. The two-by-four effect is one of the central reasons that political campaigns have become so acrimonious. The increasing mean-spiritedness of campaigns merely reflects a society where hyperbole, vulgarity, and ostentation thrive. In a Maryland senate race, William Brock III falsely suggested that Ruthann Aron, his opponent in the primary, had been convicted of fraud. Aron sued. In his defense, Brock offered this as a justification: "Everybody knows there's hyperbole in election campaigns."

In the neighboring state of Virginia, a desperate candidate for county sheriff, Ken Barnett, ran a television ad featuring side-by-side photographs of the incumbent Frank Cassell and Adolf Hitler, referred to Cassell's deputies as "goose-stepping Gestapo," and included a short scene from *Schindler's List*.

As the symbol of extreme human evil, the Nazi reference is considered an indispensable two-by-four:

- In Idaho, the state superintendent of education, Anne Fox, compared her first several weeks in office to persecution suffered by famous Nazi victim Anne Frank.

- In Washington, D.C., Mayor Marion Barry compared a federal control board to Nazis. When Speaker of the House Newt Gingrich reacted angrily to this hyperbole, a reporter pointed out how Gingrich had once compared Lyndon Johnson's Great Society to Nazism.

- New York Congressional representatives Charles Rangel and Major Owens compared the Republican Contract with America's consequences for African-Americans to the Nazis' treatment of Jews.

- In a fund-raising letter, the National Rifle Association referred to federal law enforcement officers as "jack-booted government thugs," a veiled reference to Nazi storm troopers.

- O. J. Simpson lawyer Johnnie Cochran compared police officer Mark Fuhrman to Hitler, calling him a "genocidal racist."

The two-by-four effect filters down into every aspect of our lives at home and at the office. "It's difficult to get people's attention," complains Vincent Sollitto, the communications specialist at the American Enterprise Institute. Statistics back up his familiar claim. While advertising spending per capita from 1930 to 1990 increased by 2,200 percent, polls have also shown a steep decline in message recall. "I get invitations every week," relates Sollitto, "to attend seminars from PR professionals on 'How to Make Sure Your Press Release Gets Read,' and 'How to Rise Above the Din.'" He also comes up with strategies on his own. One of his latest techniques is to both mail and fax his news releases, he explains, so as to have twice the chance of catching each target's eye. Faxing, Sollitto says, serves as a "double-catch safety net" for people too busy to open their mail.

Writers of direct-solicitation (junk) mail echo the complaint about declining attention span, though they recognize they are as much to blame as anyone. In the 1980s, junk mail grew thirteen times faster than population growth, and as the number of solicitations increased, the competition for attention heated up. "There was a time," one junk mail writer recalls wistfully, "when people would get very little other than personal mail. Now there's just a ton of junk mail, and you've got to compete with all that other stuff in the mailbox. So your outer envelope has to be very dramatic, very eye-catching, suggesting some benefit that the person might realize if they get into the envelope, whether it's lower taxes or getting rid of an old political enemy."

Two of today's favorite junk-mail techniques are the faux-personal envelope, sent without a plastic business window, and a certified letter. ("If you ever send a certified mailing," another writer confided, "the first thing you want to say is, 'I'm sorry if I caused you any inconvenience. *But this is urgent!*' Because you get a lot of people who have to drive twenty or twenty-five miles just to pick it up. Then when they find out it's junk mail, they can get pretty upset.")

The professional burdens of communications professionals and junk mail writers are merely an exaggerated version of what we all now face. Information technology has transformed the general public into a giant lay media, and in so doing, it has also bestowed upon us glutizens the quintessential media burden: to grab an audience. Everyone wants to be heard (or read or watched). If the media is now us, then we all have the same problem of seeking to get attention in a world full of glutted, distracted people. Since we are at once victims of the glut and glutizens who contribute to it, we are simultaneously casualties of the two-by-four effect and its patrons.

The two-by-four effect is especially damaging to the integrity of the news media. News outlets can't help but reward the most shameless attention-seekers. Consequently, stories on the environment and other social issues have largely come to revolve around scare tactics and crisis-mongering.

"Group Warns of Worldwide Water Crisis"
Los Angeles Times

"America's Energy Crisis Beyond the Persian Gulf"
Atlanta Constitution

"Crisis Spurs Calls for Auto Mileage Gains"
Washington Post

"Japan's Environmental 'Time Bombs'"
San Francisco Chronicle

"Pope Warns of Global Ecological Crisis"
Los Angeles Times

"Report Warns of Trash Crisis"
St. Louis Post-Dispatch

"Timber Officials Warn of Economic Crisis"
San Francisco Chronicle

Pandering to crisis-mongers is one element of the much-lamented "tabloidization of journalism," a drift toward sensationalism that is driven largely by the two-by-four effect (and is not, incidentally, limited to any particular class of journalism—part of *New Yorker* editor Tina Brown's effort to make the magazine more "relevant" in the early 1990s was to actively solicit more "outrageous" illustrations from the *New Yorker*'s stable of artists).

A raised cultural temperature can have a series of unsavory consequences. It stands to reason that the increase in sensationalism and vulgarity also leads to an increase in insults and subsequent violence. "When my husband says to someone in a parking lot that her lights are off, and she responds with 'Fuck you,' that's a real concern," says social psychologist Carol Tavris.

The two-by-four effect is also perceived as irreversible. "We can't go back and put *Ozzie & Harriet* on," says ABC network president David Westin, "and expect people to watch." If true (only time will tell for sure), this means that we are eating away, hyperbole by hyperbole, at the foundation of moderate discourse that has served this country so well over the past 200 years. The degree to which today's television programmers, movie producers, performers, spokespersons, and publishers apparently feel compelled to turn up the heat is a serious threat to moderation and intelligence in society. It reduces our attention span. It makes us numb to anything that doesn't lurch out and grab us by the throat.

As such a desensitizer, the two-by-four effect may also freeze out some of our best minds from the mainstream of public debate. If one has to be sensational and dramatic to gain attention, what does that portend for the insightful, brilliant minds whose ideas don't lend themselves to MTV videos or flashy Web pages? If our attention naturally gravitates toward the Madonnas and Howard Sterns of the world, who gets left behind in the dust? Ironically, the two-by-four effect suppresses those individuals whom we most desperately need in our complex times—the people who are willing to confront life's ambiguities.

chapter 9

Village of Babel

The stretching and splintering of culture

I n the summer of 1995, my wife and I were on vacation in Britain, enjoying not only the Royal Shakespeare Company and the Lake District but also, as it turned out, some of the most pleasant weather the region had seen in years. Hearing news updates of the record-breaking heat wave back in the States, we felt very far removed indeed from our native land.

And that's just the way we wanted it. We had traveled to the U.K. for its distinct culture and scenery. Driving aimlessly through the central lowlands of Scotland one evening, looking for a comfortable place to rest for the night, we came upon a road sign advertising the Falls of Dochart. We hadn't heard of this place—but that was good; we were after the unfamiliar. So we left primary roadway A85 and headed northeast on secondary carriageway A827. Within just a few miles, we came upon a rocky, rushing creek running right through the middle of a quaint village called Killin. The whole scene, with the Scottish mist rolling over the towering verdant glens surrounding the town, was spectacular to behold. We drove across the creek on a one-lane stone bridge and checked into a small bed and breakfast just on the other side. Then, as the light faded, we walked back across the bridge to the village pub to sample a local whisky. This was exactly the cozy and distinctly faraway setting we had dreamed about in planning our trip. American culture was safely at a distance.

Or so we thought, until we ordered our drinks and glanced up at the television. There, live from L.A. on SKY-TV, was Lance Ito refusing to meet in a sidebar with Marcia Clark, Johnnie Cochran, and the rest of the characters from the O. J. Simpson double-murder trial. Welcome to the global village. One can run but one cannot hide.

In this shrunken electronic world, CNN, MTV, and *The Wall Street Journal* want *you*—whether you happen to be in Taipei or Greenwich Village. Telephones, televisions, satellites, and computers have made great physical distances obsolete by allowing instant communication between virtually anyone, and that has led to some nearly universal cultural phenomena. National Basketball Association games are seen in more than 100 countries. Toyota cars can be purchased in 151 countries. Coca-Cola can be consumed in 185 countries—seven more countries than there are members of the United Nations. The blossoming of the World Wide Web, functioning as a global electronic library equally accessible by all who are connected, only enhances the sensation. Web pages are as varied as humanity itself and yet they are all connected to one another. With the Web, it's a small world after all—between twelve and twenty inches diagonally, depending on the size of one's computer screen.

But the global village is only one side of the coin. Recall Stanley Milgram's list of human responses to stimulus overload. Last on his list was number six: "Specialized institutions are created to absorb inputs that would otherwise swamp the individual." Indeed, the informationized world has also followed this prophecy, as can be heard with a simple glide down any American radio dial. Here we are confronted by the sounds of a severe new cultural fragmentation: from hip-hop to cool jazz to death metal to fusion to classic '60s hits to swing to grunge to public radio news to shock talk—no two stations sound even remotely alike. "It's all getting nichier and nichier now, more and more fragmented," says Lee Abrams, managing director of the ABC Satellite Radio Network. Dozens of these narrowly tailored radio formats have sprung up in the past few decades.

Channel surfing on any cable-TV system is a similarly disjointing experience, as is browsing a newsstand that features hundreds of niche magazines—from *Backpacker* to *Cigar Aficionado* to *Home Office Computing,* one or more for every vocation and avocation known to humankind. On Usenet, some 14,000 other electronic conversations are taking place simultaneously, from `alt.animals.badgers` to `rec.antiques.radio+phono`, from `rec.hunting` to `soc.bi` [sexuality]. What comes through loud and clear in these media arenas are not the cultural commonalities but the profound and, in many cases, irreconcilable, differences. As society becomes more and more virtual, the fragmentation and political polarization will only increase. In 1994, the first major political survey of Internet politics revealed, not surprisingly, a virtual world in a state of hyper-fragmentation. "Virtual communities," researchers reported, "resemble the semi-private spaces of modern health clubs more than the public spaces of agoras. . . . Instead of meeting to discuss and debate issues of common concern to the society, members of these virtual communities meet largely to promote their own interests and to reinforce their own like-mindedness. They tend to exclude anyone who disagrees. As a consequence, however, they also reinforce the fragmentation and factionalism of modern society."

From this vantage point, it appears that rather than our world becoming a cozy village, we are instead retreating into an electronic Tower of Babel, a *global skyscraper*. Instead of gathering us into the town square, the new information technology clusters us into social cubicles. There are fewer central spaces, and not even a common channel. In 1978 three television networks—ABC, CBS, and NBC—captured 90 percent of the American prime-time television viewing audience. Over the following decade, that figure dipped to 64 percent. From 1980 to 1990, while circulation dropped at general interest magazines like *Reader's Digest, Time,* and *Life,* there were nearly 3,000 new magazine startups, most of them extremely narrow in their scope. "There's really no mass media left," an ad buyer told *Forbes* magazine in 1990.

That's a gross exaggeration. Obviously, mass media still exists and, in terms of global reach, is more massive than ever before. But in practical terms, people spend more and more of their lives in narrow, specialized fields of communication. Massification of culture began in earnest with the fifteenth-century printing press, and got an enormous boost from the nineteenth-century penny press. Since the late 1960s, though, the process has been in full reverse, a communications transformation to a specialized, niche culture.

Unfolding before us, therefore, are two parallel and seemingly contradictory universes. Much of the world is indeed now tied into one massive electronic infrastructure, but the wired planet is also becoming increasingly fragmented within that wholeness. In fact, this makes perfect sense. Just as a large cocktail party breaks up into a string of small conversations—and the larger the party is, the more conversations there are—so follow the people of earth when they are thrown together into one virtual village. In order to maintain intimate communication, and in order to keep up with our own sophistication, we fragment into tiny clusters within our global skyscraper.

We specialize. In medicine, law, finance, real estate, engineering, education, and every other profession imaginable, workers have specialized their tasks to cope with the explosion of information. Specialization is how we apply our vast knowledge to many trying challenges of the human race, how we go about improving our quality of life. By narrowing our range of interest, we are able to delve further into crucial details of an issue. As a result, we develop more effective treatments for disease, more durable materials and building designs, more comfortable and lighter-weight fabrics, and so on.

It isn't just limited to our careers. Our consumer lives have also become much more specialized, allowing us to climb more deeply into obscure hobbies and acquire exotic foods. What marketers call "nichification" is, in fact, an important part of our improving quality of life.

But there is also a big price paid. In a word, it is *separation*. "[As] the role of each medical practitioner logically narrows," one doctor writes in the *Journal of the American Medical Association*, "[there is a] tendency for compartmentalizing of patient needs, and for failure of sensitive dialogue with each patient." This, in a nutshell, is the paradox of specialization: It fuels progress, but also increases isolation.

"A House divided cannot stand," Abraham Lincoln declared in 1858. More than 100 years later, our Great Emancipator sits on a giant marble chair, content in his hallowed monument just off the banks of the Potomac River, in Washington, D.C. But if Lincoln were to turn his head 120 degrees to the right, he would be unnerved to discover that in an office building hardly more than a stone's throw across the water, the country is again being vigorously partitioned—not by guns and cannons, but this time with microprocessors. Here, at 1525 Wilson Boulevard in Alexandria, Virginia, is the headquarters for Claritas, the market research company founded by the father of niche culture, Jonathan Robbin.

In the 1970s, Claritas helped to invent what is now known as niche marketing. In niche marketing, products are positioned to appeal to a series of smaller, well-defined groups, narrowly framed by demographic data: wealthy suburban teenagers, urban professionals, retired pensioners and so on. Slogans and images are selected with these specific audiences in mind and then placed in niche media outlets each particular audience is known to frequent.

Ads for organic ice cream and environmental banking, for example, grace the pages of the socially conscious lifestyle magazine *Utne Reader.* An ad for the latest advance in dishwashers appears in *Martha Stewart Living.* Not only is the tailored sales pitch considered more editorially effective; it is also much more *cost*-effective, enabling a marketer to pay less money for a richer percentage of potential customers and to forgo the large, mass-market advertising fee. Cable TV, one cable salesman boasts, "can deliver a lot less *geo waste.*"

Because of its distinct economic advantages, niche marketing has taken the American economy by storm over the last two decades. It is so prevalent, in fact, that it's easy to forget that it's such a recent phenomenon. "Systematic consumer segmentation and 'micro-marketing' was not conceived until the 1970s," writes economist John Goss, "when theoretical, technological, and institutional innovations permitted the accumulation and management of electronic data bases on consumer behavior, the statistical analysis of vast amounts of data, and the precise geographic location of consumers for marketing purposes."

The innovations Goss speaks of all point back to Jonathan Robbin. If the beginning of the great massification of culture can be dated back to Johann Gutenberg's 1450s invention of movable type in Mainz, Germany, then its antithesis—*demassification,* futurist Alvin Toffler calls it—might well be pinpointed to the tinkerings of one American, Jonathan Robbin, in the mid-1960s. To be sure, fragmentation was inevitable in our glutted world, but someone had to come along and define the parameters. It was Robbin who first conceived that computers could be used for more than lightning-quick calculations, that they could be programmed to juxtapose enormous amounts of otherwise unwieldy data in order to achieve a new degree of pattern recognition. Out of this, niche culture was born.

Actually, the Jonathan Robbin odyssey began long before Robbin himself got directly involved. In 1946 the very first computer, the Electronic Numerical Integrator and Calculator, or ENIAC, was designed for the U.S. military so that it could improve its missile trajectory calculations. This colossus consisted of 18,000 vacuum tubes, 6,000 switches, 10,000 capacitors, 70,000 resistors, and 1,500 relays, and it took up 1,800 square feet of space. The payoff, though, was huge. It could make an amazing 5,000 calculations per second—a thousand times faster than any previous calculator.

Such astonishing quickness drew the immediate attention of the U.S. Census Bureau, which, in 1951, acquired ENIAC's offspring, UNIVAC (Universal Automatic Computer), in order to improve the tabulation of census data. Even after the 1960 census, though, UNIVAC was employed merely as a labor-saving device, an extremely powerful calculator that could add, subtract, list, and file information much faster than human hands. No one in the Census Bureau yet recognized that their machine had the capability to do much, much more for them than quick tabulations.

In 1964 Lyndon Johnson launched the War on Poverty. Before the Office of Economic Opportunity (OEO) could begin implementing the web of social welfare programs, however, it faced the monumental task of mapping out a detailed demographic study of all Americans and their economic means—coordinating data from dozens of government agencies, including the Census Bureau. For this, OEO recruited Robbin, a "human ecologist" trained in the study of the social habits of human populations. Robbin had already started to use computers for what was known in his field as large-scale multivariate statistical analysis. For the OEO, he wrote programs to interlace information from all twenty-nine separate agencies and turn it into detailed socioeconomic comparisons of every *tract* in the U.S.—units of about 1,500 households each, which were the Census Department's best approximation of U.S. neighborhoods at the time.

The result was the first-ever accessible collection of data on American neighborhoods and their relative affluence, degree of mobility, particular ethnicity, level of urbanization, and type of housing. It was not only a great technical achievement, but also a broad analytical breakthrough demonstrating that carving up a nation into tens of thousands of tiny slivers can be an extraordinarily effective way of understanding the unit as a whole.

It was also an entrepreneurial bonanza. "I reduced something like a billion pieces of information from the federal census efforts into forty types of neighborhoods," Robbin now boasts. "That made it possible for humans to encompass these things to use them in real marketing actions to make real money with them, and to go forward in life." In 1971 Robbin established a company called Claritas (Latin for "clarity") to test his hunch that he was on the verge of developing an entirely new genre of consumer market database in which lifestyle types could be detected, fleshed out, and exploited by the private sector. It was a chance to take market demographics past cumbersome and ineffectual cross-tabulating, a crude method of breaking large survey samples into tiny fragments based on age, sex, ethnicity, and so on. Unless the original survey group was enormous, cross-tabbing was fated to measure data based on subgroups so small that the whole procedure was almost statistically worthless.

In 1976 Robbin introduced his landmark PRIZM database, the first comprehensive geodemographic analysis ever. ("Just as a prism breaks light into a spectrum of its component parts, PRIZM reveals any consumer market as a colorful array of the distinct neighborhood types that compose the market.") Through elegant and exhaustively refined algorithms, PRIZM excavated the statistically relevant similarities between localities. Neighborhoods scattered across the nation that never could have been so definitively categorized using pre-computer methods of analysis, were gathered together and put under a single "lifestyle" category. Molalla, Oregon, and Moravia, New York, are both "Shotguns & Pickups," stocked with predominantly large families, skilled craftspersons, and sport hunters, while "Pools & Patio" towns Mission, Kansas, and Fairfield, Connecticut, contain older, prosperous, white-collar empty-nesters with a penchant for golf and Sunday barbecues. In all, forty lifestyle types emerged, and almost every community in the nation was put into one of these categories. "These basic clusters were tested, refined, and calibrated with actual consumer purchase data.

Behavioral tests and enhancements to PRIZM tapped millions of consumer purchase records from multiple sources covering auto buyers, magazine subscribers, real estate transactions, consumer credit, direct marketing response, and consumer expenditure data."

The final step in this computer-fueled lifestyle analysis was to put an accessible face on these lifestyle clusters. This task fell to marketing whiz Robin Page, who was recruited into Claritas to give zippy names and descriptions to each cluster—Money & Brains, Rank & File, Hispanic Mix, and so on. A new age of computer-driven niche marketing was born.

Claritas's forty American lifestyle clusters, 1976

BLUE-BLOOD ESTATES–America's wealthiest

MONEY & BRAINS–Posh urban enclaves

FURS & STATION WAGONS–New Money suburbs

URBAN GOLD COAST–Upscale high-rises

POOLS & PATIOS–Older, upper-middle-class suburbs

TWO MORE RUNGS–Comfortable, multi-ethnic suburbs

YOUNG INFLUENTIALS–Yuppies

YOUNG SUBURBIA–Young families

GOD'S COUNTRY–Upscale frontier boomtowns

BLUE-CHIP BLUES–Wealthiest blue-collar suburbs

BOHEMIAN MIX–Inner-city bohemians

LEVITTOWN, USA–Aging post–World War II subdivisions

GRAY POWER–Upper middle-class retirement

BLACK ENTERPRISE–African-American middle and upper-middle class

NEW BEGINNINGS–Fringe-city singles complexes

BLUE-COLLAR NURSERY–Middle-class young family towns

NEW HOMESTEADERS–Exurban boom towns of young families

NEW MELTING POT–New-immigrant neighborhoods

TOWNS & GOWNS–College

RANK & FILE–Older, blue-collar, industrial

MIDDLE AMERICA–Midsize towns

OLD YANKEE ROWS–Working class

COALBURB & CORNTOWN–Industrial

SHOTGUNS & PICKUPS–Lumber and agricultural villages

GOLDEN PONDS–Rustic cottages near mountains and lakes

AGRI-BUSINESS–Farm towns

EMERGENT MINORITIES–African-American urban working class

SINGLE CITY BLUES–Downscale urban singles

MINES & MILLS–Struggling steel and mining towns

BACK-COUNTRY FOLKS–Remote downscale farm towns

NORMA RAE–VILLE–Lower-middle-class mill towns

SMALLTOWN DOWNTOWN–Inner cities of small industrial cities

GRAIN BELT–Sparsely populated rural areas

HEAVY INDUSTRY–Lower working class

SHARE CROPPERS–Southern agricultural hamlets

DOWNTOWN DIXIE STYLE–Aging Southern African-American neighborhoods

HISPANIC MIX–Barrios

TOBACCO ROADS–African-American farmworkers

HARD SCRABBLE–Poorest rural areas

PUBLIC ASSISTANCE–Inner-city ghettos

Here's an example of how PRIZM might be used. An American distributor of the rich, hoppy German beer Räumtrupp wishes to expand its customer base. Naturally, the primary questions are:

1. Who is most likely to pay a premium for this refined brew?
2. How can these people best be contacted?

PRIZM's database already contains the several lifestyle types known to enjoy imported beer. The database also reveals that these probable customers live in the neighborhoods it calls Blue-Blood

Estates, Urban Gold Coast, and Bohemian Mix. It might also stand a good chance with Towns & Gowns, but is bound to fail with New Homesteaders, Mines & Mills, or Shotguns & Pickups. Here's a map of where these target neighborhoods are; here's a list of the TV programs each niche group enjoys, the radio stations they listen to, the magazines they subscribe to. And, oh yes, here are their *addresses*.

In delving into this level of demographic and consumer detail, classifying each sliver and helping to devise specific appeals for each lifestyle, Claritas not only identifies an ever-fragmenting world. *It celebrates it and helps perpetuate it*. "There are very few products or brand names that still enjoy broad, unanimous appeal," boasts a recent company brochure. "Precise target marketing technologies help marketers take advantage of rapid changes by targeting the appropriate 'fragments' and turning them into successful 'niches.'" Claritas's influence in actually further nichifying society is perhaps best illustrated by the fact that their number of identifiable clusters has now increased from forty to *sixty-two*. If Claritas's analysis is to be believed, as it clearly is every day by hundreds of companies who pay handsomely for the information, our nation has experienced a dramatic increase in its "lifestyle" types over the course of a mere two decades.

Soon after PRIZM and similar systems were introduced in the 1970s, it became clear that niche marketing was not going to be limited to Snickers bars and salad dressing. In 1978 a Washington campaign consultant named Matt Reese caught wind of PRIZM and managed to acquire the exclusive political rights to it. On his very first test run with the program, Reese successfully thwarted a Missouri antilabor referendum, coming from thirty-three points behind to win by ten points. "This system was magic," he says. "It was an opportunity to segregate the voting population intelligently and precisely."

PRIZM and niche marketing, says Reese, turned campaign economics on its head. Up to that point, all campaigns were drowning in *geo waste*. "Pollster Peter Hart may give me a poll that says that Catholic women over fifty are my target—but I don't know where

Catholic women over fifty are. I can only reach them with very expensive mass media television. So I'm talking to a million people in order to find 50,000. That's pretty wasteful. With geodemographics, I can tell within a four-square-block area—280 households—what kind of folks live there and what they think." Today Reese's late-'70s success with PRIZM's geodemographics is considered an American political watershed. Campaign strategists now accept it as industry gospel that, as they put it, they are much better off shooting with a rifle than with a shotgun.

Unfortunately for the rest of us, the brutality of this gun metaphor is more apropos than most campaign professionals realize. By identifying, exaggerating, and constantly highlighting stereotypical social characteristics, niche marketing coerces people into staying in their social cocoons. "Geodemographics display a strategic intent to control social life," John Goss concludes darkly. For the sake of market convenience and profitability, society is imbued with messages conditioning it to stay neatly subdivided into distinct consumer categories.

Ultimately, nichification is not just about the precise division of electronic communities by interest, but also by time schedule. Bill Gates has defined this phase of the information revolution as a shift from a "synchronous" world, where events occur according to one unified national schedule, à la *TV Guide*, to an *asynchronous* one, where all manner of information, communication, and entertainment is available to everyone at all times—a video-on-demand culture. Just as the answering machine replaced the restriction of having to reach someone live on the other end of a phone with the option of leaving a recorded message at any hour of the day, we will soon leave behind rigid schedules in favor of an endless array of scheduling options. In his highly optimistic book, *The Road Ahead,* Gates describes the shift in wonderfully liberating terms:

> Once you make a form of communication asynchronous, you can also increase the variety and selection possibilities. . . . The highway will enable capabilities that seem magical when they

are described, but represent technology at work to make our lives easier and better. . . . You indicate what you want, and presto! you get it.

As it makes life ever more convenient, though, this super-efficient asynchronous-niche capitalism comes at an enormous cost to society at large. For when the world becomes so profoundly splintered into distinct consumer tribes, humankind begins to lose the most valuable thing it has ever had: common information and shared understanding.

A scientist was examining the leeches in
a marsh when Zarathustra, the prophet,
approached him and asked if he was
a specialist in the ways of the leech.
"O, Zarathustra, . . . that would be
something immense; how could I
presume to do so! . . . That, however,
of which I am master and knower, is the
brain of the leech; that is my world! . . .
For the sake of this did I cast
everything else aside, for the sake
of this did everything else
become indifferent to me . . . "

—Friedrich Nietzsche, *Thus Spake Zarathustra*

chapter 10

A Nation of Lonely Molecules

*F*or the sake of this did everything else become indifferent to me. . . . This is our postmodern refrain. Professional specialization and consumer nichification encroach upon our common culture. Rather than a healthy swirl of communication among citizens of different backgrounds and perspectives, we are left with a hyper-efficient communications infrastructure that not only highlights social distinctions; it fortifies them.

The Eighth Law of Data Smog (Goss's Law)
Birds of a feather flock virtually together.

("Of course we're becoming more fragmented," a journalist colleague said to me matter-of-factly one afternoon in my office as I

*LINKED-IN
TOO?
↑
↓
NOT
WHETHER
TOTAL LI
POP ≈
ACTUAL POP,
BUT WHETHER
NETWKS/REL
ARE DIVERSE
WITHIN*

summarized the issues in this book. "That's why all people at parties can talk about anymore is sports and movies.")

Andy Warhol had it partly right: In the future, we will all be famous for fifteen minutes—but only within our extremely specialized communities. Surveys tend to bear this out, revealing not ignorance, per se, but a severe crisis in common information. Like minds stay in touch with one another, but not with the community at large, as nichification supplies *insulation* along with communication. "There is so much information," laments pollster Andrew Kohut, "that in some sense, people throw their hands up and say, 'Well, I'm going to focus on this very narrow part of the world.' People who used to read *Life* and *Look* magazine in the '50s now are great experts at motorcycles and spend a lot of time reading *Motorcycle World.* And what happens on the cover of *Life* and *Look* comparably is missed."

When I visited FCC chairman James Quello in his office to discuss alarming knowledge surveys, his response was, "There's so much news and news analysis about. It seems to me that if people would just tune in, they'd be better informed than that." The problem, of course, is that people *are* tuning in and becoming informed—but they're tuning into niche media and they're acquiring specialized knowledge. As our information supply increases, our common discourse and shared understanding decrease. Technically, we possess an unprecedented amount of information; however, what is commonly known has dwindled to a smaller and smaller percentage every year. This should be a sobering realization for a democratic nation, a society that must share information in order to remain a union.

This doesn't mean things are getting worse for democracy. But it does mean that our contemporary social goal of achieving a truly just society has a surprising impediment built right in.

This helps explain the stagnation in American political knowledge over the last fifty years, even as Americans were formally educated to an unprecedented degree. We face a paradox of abundance-induced amnesia. The more information we come upon, the more we narrow our focus. The more we know, the less we know. The vicious spiral drives a growing wedge between people within different spheres of knowledge. We are, as Earl Shorris says, "A nation of lonely molecules."

> Specialization makes sleepwalkers of us all; the global village predicted by the seers of the 1960's is being replaced by electronic cottages populated by isolated dreamers. We do not know our neighbors. If we are financial experts, we are speechless in the presence of research chemists; if we are scholars, we cannot make out the grimaces of merchants. We are a nation of lonely molecules.
>
> —Earl Shorris, *A Nation of Salesmen*

With the Internet, this trend is exaggerated. Eleven billion words and 22 million Web pages bring us more information than ever before and, because of this, less information *shared*. Like niche radio and cable TV, the Net encourages a cultural splintering that can render physical communities much less relevant and free people from having to climb outside their own biases, assumptions, inherited ways of thought. This is perhaps best evidenced by the ominous emergence of so-called smart agents, which automatically filter out information deemed irrelevant to the customer. IBM's InfoSage, for example, boasts that it "brings only the news and information you want to read right to your desktop. . . . based on a personal profile you create, our sophisticated search technology probes over 2,200 sources and delivers articles related only to your topics."

While filtering mechanisms are an increasingly necessary part of life in the information society, automated smart agents like InfoSage pose a great danger, precisely because they are so effective at weeding out unwanted information. Imagine having a butler who was under strict instructions to turn away all phone callers and visitors whose names were not on his screening list. You would succeed in limiting your contacts with people, but at the cost of never making any new acquaintances. In similar fashion, smart agents manage the information glut by eliminating serendipitous information from our lives. Accidentally stumbling onto entirely new and interesting subject matter, common in a conventional library, becomes much less likely in a customized-information environment. (Nicholas Negroponte insists that smart agents can and should include an adjustable "serendipity dial," but one cannot automate spontaneity.) This severely limits much of what it means to be human in a free, liberal society in which shared ideas and experience is vital. Such a restriction is tantamount to constructing one's own information prison. We must make an effort to avoid filters like InfoSage that all-too-neatly apportion us into sealed information cubicles. Instead of delegating filtering to automatic smart agents, we should make our own decisions, act as our own filters.

Unless we do, technology will lead us in the other direction, toward narrower worlds where information is tailored to our specific professional, cultural, political, and leisurely interests. We will spend even less time watching the nightly news, reading the big-city paper.[*] We will spend even less time interacting with people outside our range of interests. Indeed, even those forums that appear to be projecting an image of ubiquity may be more of a global village mirage than the real thing. *Reader's Digest,* for example—the epitome of the general interest magazine—is also quietly going niche. They have commissioned Claritas to develop the means to distribute *different* editions to each of PRIZM's sixty-two different lifestyle segments.

Let us remember that a world of tribes, subcultures, and clans can be invigorating, and nichification has been a great gift to many people. Previously "disenfranchised" societies are empowered by new technologies allowing them to communicate cheaply and with-

---

[*] James Fallows points out that the sharp decline in general newspapers has been largely driven by the rise in niche retailing. He writes: "Over the last three decades, retailing and publishing alike have steadily narrowed and refined their focus, to reach more carefully selected subgroups of a more segmented American population . . . As the traditional retailers have suffered, so have the newspapers, for which they were usually the biggest advertisers. Specialized shops have found more efficient ways to reach the customers they are looking for, from targeted catalogue marketing to infomercials on cable TV."

out geographic limitation. Gays and lesbians, for example, who are inherently dispersed throughout society, have benefited tremendously from online forums that provide them with the opportunity to share their intimate thoughts about what it means to be gay, practical considerations about living a healthy, happy life, and ways to band together and force politicians to take them seriously as a group of citizens with important interests. The same can be said of the opportunities afforded to linguists, Latinos, teenagers, environmentalists, ethicists, folklorists, engineers, documentarians, therapists, movie buffs, studio musicians, plumbers, and freelance writers. Being able to share one's personal thoughts, ambitions, accomplishments, trials, and tribulations with other like-minded people is part of the joy of being human.

Nichification also has less vital but still meaningful benefits. The general population enjoys access to a much wider variety of foods, music, theater, film, and other crafts than in any time in our history. We are richer for the ability to interact with thousands of subcultures in our midst.

But there is a great danger here of mistaking cultural tribalism for real, shared understanding. It is one thing to dine in Morocco, or in a surrogate Morocco in Greenwich Village, and quite another to share with Moroccans the responsibility of maintaining a democratic community. A pluralistic democracy requires a certain amount of tolerance and consensus, rooted in the ability to understand a wide variety of perspectives and agree on common questions. In this country, we increasingly speak very different languages and different dialects of the same language. We share fewer metaphors, icons, historical interests, and current news events. Bill Gates's celebrated "asynchrony" is but an eloquent way of saying that in our new electronic world of endless communication options, we are "out of synch" with one another.

The Net helps exclusive groups come together to form an even tighter bond. Communities tend to be naturally inclusive. In so doing, it fosters not communities, as many like to claim, but far more limited microcultures. (Some proponents of the World Wide

Web strongly take issue with this interpretation, arguing that the Web, with its hyperlinking structure, actually encourages interdisciplinary thought and broad, multicultural communication. After all, any Web surfer can go from the Contract with America to Ansel Adams photographs to World War II history in a matter of a few clicks of a mouse. While it is true that Web-browsing allows for an extremely diverse information experience, the end result is still very much a situation of extreme nichification in which Web surfers are encouraged to explore their personal range of interests and are rewarded with highly specific information on those interests—as well as electronic interactions with people who share those interests.)

In this way, nichification and "asynchrony" are underlying reasons for the troubling level of social polarization plaguing the United States in modern times, the nasty disagreements and seeming inability of people to come together to form consensus on important issues. "When was the last time you talked about race with someone of a different race?" Bill Bradley is fond of asking civic groups in his speeches. "If the answer is never, you're part of the problem." His implication, that we're losing touch with one another and that it is driving our pluralistic society into the ground, is partly a function of information technology. *Can't we all get along?* Under such fragmented conditions, without a *lingua franca,* maybe not.

The anxiety caused by this cultural Balkanization has led to a palpable yearning for someone to ride into the White House on a white horse and make us whole again. We desperately want to belong to something larger than our families, local communities, and vocational clubs. We viscerally need to belong to a nation. And when we feel detached, as many do now, it is upsetting. The 1996 groundswell for Colin Powell was rooted in the faith that the general's moral convictions, sharp decisiveness, and quiet decency would inspire a sweeping coalition of divergent interests. "I see him as one of the last chances we have to try and unite our country again and stop all this polarization and splintering and fracturing," declared Ernest Watson, leader of Draft Colin Powell's North Carolina chapter.

Other presidential contenders spoke during the '96 campaign of the importance of unity. President Clinton declared that "we can't restore the American dream unless we can find some way to bring the American people closer together." Bob Dole adopted an English-first plank on the grounds that "we need the glue of language to help hold us together." But any leader is going to find cohesiveness an increasingly difficult challenge. The fragmentation of consumer culture has co-opted our political culture. "Leadership is harder in an age of decentralized media," opines Robert Wright. "In the old days, a president could give a prime-time talk on all three networks and know that he had everyone's attention. But this sort of forum is disappearing as conservatives watch National Empowerment Television, nature buffs watch the Discovery Channel, sports fans watch ESPN."

After two centuries of vigilance, it is almost surreal to imagine that the republic will suffer mortal blows from cable television. But the power of this splintering technology should not be underestimated. The "geo waste" that niche marketing helps marketers avoid is also another phrase for *shared discourse,* something we desperately need to support our pluralistic culture. Somewhere along the line, we seem to have inadvertently constructed an information economy that works directly against crucial democratic tenets.

There is in our future a TV or Internet
populism, in which the emotional
response of a selected group of citizens
can be presented and accepted as the
Voice of the People.

—Umberto Eco

chapter 11

Superdemocracy

COLORADO SPRINGS—In a small conference room on the
mezzanine of the sprawling Broadmoor Hotel, software en-
trepreneur and political revolutionary Tim Stryker is laying
out the spooky details of his electronic insurrection with a
laptop and an overhead projector. His radical plan, called
"Superdemocracy," is to replace representative democracy in the
U.S. with a form of computer-assisted *direct* democracy—or, as this
computer technician with twenty-four years' experience puts it, "a
continuous, networked hierarchy of online referenda, open to all."

Stryker is not the first to suggest that breakthroughs in information technology enable a progressive democratic transformation. In
1992 Ross Perot famously touted the "electronic town hall" as the
solution to our country's problems. The deficit issue is a good
example of something that Perot thought could be explained to
people over cyberspace and subsequently solved through a series of
electronic referenda. He explained: "The people will say, 'All right,

the responsible thing to do is to raise taxes on ourselves.' And that leads to the next question: What should the tax system be? . . . It would be conceived, worked out, and agreed to by the American people through the town hall."

The linchpin of Perot's plan is a citizenry that is not only intelligent and means well, but also has sufficient time and energy to master difficult environmental, economic, and defense issues. "If we ever put the people back in charge of this country and make sure they understand the issues," he has insisted, "you'll see the White House and Congress, like a ballet, pirouetting around the stage getting it done in unison." To prove his trust in the system he was proposing, Perot declared that, as president, he would happily let himself be subject to instant electronic recall. "I would just go through the town hall. I'd say, 'Now, would you be happier if someone replaced me?' If the answer came back 'Yes,' then I would say, 'That's fine.'"

Stryker's plan is equally sanguine about the ability of the people to rule themselves directly, given the right infrastructure. He has outlined perhaps the most ambitious and specific blueprint, calling for the replacement of the judicial and legislative branches of the U.S. government with a never-ending series of plebiscites, in which each citizen would have voting power on every piece of proposed legislation and a part in every verdict in every relevant trial.

> You come home from the office after a hard day's work, kick your shoes off, and, flipping on the tube, decide to take a quick glance at the city's pending resolutions. You notice that today is the last day to vote on the street-repair proposal, the referendum on funding low-income housing on the north side of town, and the decision whether or not to permit someone named John Hosiger to operate a liquor store downtown. The display shows you the votes that your proxy, Sharon Imeld, will cast for you if you don't do anything. Sharon's already fine on the street-repair thing, but she's way off base on the low-income housing issue, so you override her there. . . . You pop over to Trials . . . Up for decision today are Blanche Newald,

accused of grand larceny, and Abe Newman, 2nd-degree manslaughter. You select Abe's case and begin poring through the state's evidence and the defense's counterpoints . . .

The details confirm any skeptic's worst suspicions: Stryker's plan is as preposterous as it is ambitious. The notion that citizens of such an enormously complex nation as the United States would be able to develop the necessary expertise to make informed decisions on every aspect of governance is terribly unrealistic, as is the confidence that direct votes would completely obviate the need for coordination and consensus-building.

Given these deficiencies, the good news is this: Superdemocracy, in all its complexity, will never ever be adopted, mostly because our American Constitution protects minorities from the tyranny of the majority.

The very bad news, however, is that, in their depictions of a society where popular sentiment is electronically monitored and swiftly translated into public policy, Stryker and Perot unknowingly describe a revolution that has largely already taken place—much to our detriment. In a very real sense, superdemocracy has already arrived, and it is not so super.

One of the most commonly heard criticisms of the federal government today is that it is "out of touch." Technically speaking, though, this couldn't be further from the truth. Congress and the White House receive record levels of direct input from the citizenry via phone, fax, e-mail and U.S. postal "snail mail." (In 1970 Congress received 15 million pieces of mail. In 1991 it received over 300 million pieces.) Since the 1950s, information technology has all but eliminated the communicative distance between representatives and ordinary citizens. Long-distance telephone calls have become so affordable that a short call of complaint or support is now of negligible cost to most Americans. The fax machine combines the power of the instantaneous phone call with the articulation of the written letter. Most recently, the convenience and cost-effectiveness of e-mail has raised the volume considerably.

Advances in communication have dramatically transformed lobbying from an elite corporate perk into a facet of ordinary citizenship. The American Association of Retired Persons, for example, has grown to comprise more than 30 million members, one out of every six adult Americans. "Almost every American who reads these words is a member of a lobby," writes Jonathan Rauch in *Demosclerosis,* a book that explores the underpinnings of political gridlock. "We have met the special interests, and they are us." In addition, a new form of lobbying, dubbed "grassroots lobbying," has also sprung up to take advantage of the quick and cheap communications. Grassroots lobbyists use phone banks, direct mail, and computer networks to incite large numbers of ordinary citizens into phoning, faxing, and e-mailing their representatives about issues currently in play. The idea is to generate direct political pressure on a representative in order to show him or her that, come reelection time, here are tens of thousands of voters who will remember which way a certain vote came down.

One such lobbying effort by a consortium of long-distance phone companies, for example, involved 500 phone operators contacting consumers all across the country to ask them if they were in favor of competition in the local phone market. Anyone responding "yes" to this question was then asked to authorize telegrams sent in his or her name to a number of key representatives in Congress about impending telecommunications legislation. This massive operation generated over half a million telegrams sent to Capitol Hill in just ten days. Constitutionally speaking, nothing has changed. Politicians still retain the technical freedom to vote their conscience. But in practical terms, these high-speed communications advances make it much more difficult for them to resist the whims of their constituents.

Still, this speedier, purer democracy has been an enormous political boon in several important ways. Faxes, cable television, and modems have rendered the infamous smoke-filled room a thing of the past, transforming post-Watergate America into a thoroughly documented, well-monitored public sphere. With committee meetings broadcast on C-SPAN and campaign financing information posted on the World Wide Web, today's politicians are cleaner, more selfless, better educated, more responsive than ever before in history. The ethical standards of our public servants, says the Brookings Institution's Thomas Mann, are "probably as high as they have ever been."

The emergence of niche culture has also turned the tables on political alienation. When information media was expensive and scarce, it tended to be owned and operated exclusively for the pleasure of the majority culture and the wealthy, leaving poor, minority groups with the difficult choice of conforming or remaining excluded. As long as this held true, entire subcultures remained invisible to the world and to each other. Now, as we have seen, the formerly invisible are putting out their own 'zines, listservs, Websites, and cable TV shows.

The downside of our newly electronic democracy, though, is that our leaders' ears are so close to the ground, they sometimes find it difficult to lead.

> BOB EDWARDS: What's the Senate's chief concern [about Somalia]?
>
> COKIE ROBERTS: Well, its chief concern is public opinion. What they're hearing from home is, "Bring our boys and girls back." And I must tell you that the polling numbers continue to show that the president's policy is simply not selling with the American people. . . . The president's overall handling of foreign policy in the course of a month has flipped from more than 50 percent approving of it to more than 50 percent disapproving of it. . . . So, the Senate's looking at all of that and responding.
>
> —From National Public Radio's *Morning Edition*

In Washington, D.C., this tyranny of public opinion is known as the CNN Effect, the fatalistic perception that the American people are so plugged-in that it would be political suicide for leaders to

from popular opinion. "People in the White House turn on the
~ion, and they say, 'Oh my god, the American public is seeing
~ff!'" laments pollster Andrew Kohut. While this immediacy
uoes motivate politicians to keep their noses clean, it also stifles
leadership. Out of fear, political leaders act according to perceived
public opinion rather than "getting out in front" of their constituents.

This fear is generated not only by the information-immediacy,
but also by political pollsters who have elevated *followership* to a science by helping politicians fashion policies based on what's most
popular at any given time. These pollsters find out what people
want to hear, and then they help their clients say it. Throughout
the 1990s, both parties have excelled at this practice. In 1992 Bill
Clinton adopted poll-driven positions with an extraordinary degree
of effectiveness, employing an agenda that, on the one hand, ener-
gized the traditional democratic base of blue-collar workers and environmentalists while at the same time luring "swing" voters with
promises of a middle-class tax cut. Clinton also proved to be perhaps the greatest practitioner ever of geodemographic fragmented
politics, saying different things to different regions of the country
and to various niche groups.

Not to be outdone in the realm of followership, Republicans in
1994 contracted conservative pollster Frank Luntz to put together a
Contract with America, a document synthesized by conservative
pollster Frank Luntz and then–minority whip Newt Gingrich according to the most popular Republican ideas at the time.

Thus the ready availability of accurate polling data has the unfortunate effect of turning politicians into unwitting chameleons.
"The scientific methodology of contemporary opinion research,"
Suzannah Lessard writes in *The Washington Monthly,* "raises a form
of enslavement that is restricting and soul-destroying to degrees
hitherto unknown. Before, politicians had to guess what people
wanted . . . that uncertainty creates an opening for taking a position
closer to one's convictions. Under current conditions, however,
there is almost no uncertainty." Would-be leaders' minds, Lessard
says, are "colonized" by polling technology.

Followership wouldn't be such a bad thing if Americans were capable of making leadership-quality decisions. But, generally speaking, we citizens are simply too busy with our own complex, harried lives to also excel at making key policy decisions. Therefore, we have an unfortunate coinciding of two consequences of technology: more citizen power with less citizen understanding.

The Ninth Law of Data Smog

The electronic town hall allows for speedy communication and bad decision-making.

Tim Stryker's dream of a purer democracy, as enabled by the information revolution, is paradoxically subverted by the very same technology: People have more of a voice, but—with the increasing complexity and fragmentation of society—less and less of an ability to self-govern. As our personal lives become richer, more specialized, and more complex, we are left with even less time to sort out the particulars of welfare or any other policy.

So, while critics carp that government is unresponsive to the people, the problem is in fact precisely the opposite: Government is *all too responsive* to a citizenry that cannot—and should not be expected to—absorb and reflect on all of the details of governance. Representative democracy works best when informed citizens elect courageous representatives who take strong moral cues from constituents but are also unafraid to occasionally step out in front of public opinion, to make tough decisions that will aid the country in the long run. Just because we now have the technological capability to institute Ross Perot's electronic town hall doesn't mean that we should adopt such a system. Our true political salvation is decidedly lower tech: We as citizens need to find, nominate, and elect great leaders.

PART 3

A New Order

Whether it's about agency billings and income or high-stakes geopolitical strategy, disinformation is part of the communications arsenal. Efforts to confuse, misdirect, mislead, or confound a public are part of today's world.

—*Advertising Age*

chapter 12

Creatures from the Info Lagoon

From out of the info bog, several vibrant (and virulent) new life forms emerge. The anarchy created by information glut is an extremely hospitable environment to a medley of vile creatures. To them, data smog is not a vexing problem, but a fresh opportunity.

Exactly who benefits most is the subject of much debate. Poking around cyberspace one day, I happened on one of the many clever back-and-forth electronic discussions on the subject, a duel of exaggerated dystopian visions of society after the information revolution. Projecting the worst-case scenario can be just as much fun as projecting the best, and can also serve the public by vividly alerting them to real dangers.

The first dark vision, offered by TCMay@got.net, was that of a world where information is so chaotic and "free" that criminals will be guaranteed anonymity and will roam the virtual landscape doing horrible deeds without fear of being caught, pillaging people's electronic files, threatening the integrity of our new information infrastructure. The combination of nearly unbreakable cryptography and a glutted, untraceable information universe, TCMay argued in his "Crypto Anarchist Manifesto," will stymie tomorrow's Scotland Yard, FBI, and National Security Agency.

> . . . crypto anarchy will allow national secrets to be traded freely and will allow illicit and stolen materials to be traded. . . . Just as the technology of printing altered and reduced the power of medieval guilds and the social power structure, so too will cryptologic methods fundamentally alter the nature of corporations and of government interference in economic transactions.

Cryptology is the practice of coded language, enabling two or more people to reliably share military, political, business, and personal secrets in messages passed in public forums. It has been a part of humanity as long as secrets have. The earliest known written cryptography dates back to nonstandard Egyptian hieroglyphs inscribed in 1900 B.C. Around 500 B.C., Hebrew scribes recorded the Book of Jeremiah in an alphabet-substitution cipher now known as ATBASH. In the 1790s, Thomas Jefferson invented a wheel cipher that was used, in updated form, by U.S. Navy boats in World War II.

In the 1990s, a sophisticated mathematics-based cryptographic program became available for free to anyone with a computer. The software, PGP (Pretty Good Privacy), is considered virtually uncrackable. (Try it yourself: download the program at www.commtouch.com/uspgp.htm.) As TCMay suggests, cryptography now affords an unprecedented buffer of privacy to virtually anyone who wants it. For businesses and governments trying to protect important secrets, this is a very good thing. But the same technology keeping U.S. military codes secure also allows ne'er-do-wells to keep criminal actions more secure than ever before in history. TCMay believes that this one technology could single-handedly cripple American democracy by allowing financial transactions to take place away from the eyes of the IRS.

Naturally, this has the FBI and other law enforcement agencies worried. In 1993 the Clinton administration proposed a solution: a national standard for encryption that would allow the government to keep a special decoding key in escrow, usable with permission from a government review agency. This "clipper chip" would effectively extend the type of surveillance power currently enjoyed by police into the computer age. The proposal was lambasted by the libertarian-minded Internet community because of its potential for government abuse. Criminals, the protesters argued, will still have their unbreakable encryption software, while under this proposal the rest of us law-abiding citizens would be subject to unwarranted governmental intrusion; to give any government a golden key into all of our personal and professional communication would be to invite a creeping invasion of privacy and unprecedented incursions into our liberty. In 1994 the largest electronic petition in history, listing 47,000 people who opposed key escrow, was delivered to the White House.

How much to fear the rogue element and how much to fear the government? Having to reformulate policy on this age-old question is further complicated by a third major privacy concern, which was articulated by the other dystopian vision I came across on the Net. In "The Un-Encrypted Consumer's Manifesto," Douganews@aol.com argued that the biggest worry is, in a sense, just the opposite of TCMay's: There isn't too much privacy, but far too little. As purchase data becomes more and more accessible via computers, Douganews pointed out, we consumers will be open books for corporations and politicians to read, analyze and manipulate. Thanks to Jonathan Robbin and his fellow geodemographic practitioners, the most important information around now is nothing that anyone has ever bothered to keep secret in the history of humankind—nor ever could. This technology, he said, presents

> . . . an unprecedented opportunity for companies to observe
> and collect precise information about potential customers.
> Every time we go on line, our computers are looking at us

too. . . . While the Crypto-minority will be moving information, currency and assassination plots around the globe, the
majority of us average Joes will be subscribers to mainstream
online service providers. We will be wrapping our demographic
profiles, spending habits, secret longings, and private thoughts
into a neat little package, and we'll pay our service providers an
hourly wage to observe us while we wrap it.

I found this playful exchange to be remarkably insightful into
the paradoxical nature of our evolving technology. TCMay and
Douganews are each correct. Information anarchy is equally fit to
serve the crafty thief and the ambitious salesperson.

The exciting new criminal and terrorist opportunities are the
subject for another book. In this section we will explore the latter
concern—the fresh opportunities for *legal* abuse and power-grab-
bing afforded by the information glut.

> The telescreen received and transmitted
> simultaneously. . . . There was no way of
> knowing whether you were being
> watched at any given moment.

—George Orwell, *Nineteen Eighty-Four*

chapter 13

Dataveillance

Orwell had it partly right. Technology has made direct surveillance so easy and cheap that virtually no one is safe from electronic snoops. There was the McDonald's manager in New York whose "private" voice mail messages from his secret lover were intercepted by management and played for his wife. . . . There was the journalist who sat down to her terminal one day and began to sketch out a first draft of her story when—from out of nowhere—a sentence appeared on her computer monitor that she had not written: *I don't like that lead!* It was her editor, taking an unsolicited look-see from another floor in the building. . . . There is Ron Edens, founder of Electronic Banking Systems, a direct-mail donation processor, who tracks his data-entry clerks not only by keystroke and error-rate (a minimum of 8,500 correct strokes required per hour, or the ax), but also with eight hidden video cameras from his office. "There's a little bit of Sneaky Pete to it," he brags, adding: "It's easier from behind, because they don't know you're watching."

But these bone-chilling anecdotes from the workplace tell only a small part of the modern surveillance story. They don't even begin to convey the vast scope of *dataveillance,* the massive collection and distillation of consumer data into a hyper-sophisticated brand of marketing analysis.

The legacy of Jonathan Robbin's geodemographic revolution of the 1960s and '70s is that Big Brother now has a crew of data sweepers, and that there's no such thing anymore as innocuous information. What once might have been considered harmless personal trivia—which videos you rented this week, whether you like starch in your laundered shirts, whether you buy name-brand or generic aspirin—can today all be turned into useful intelligence by powerful cross-referencing databases; what to mere mortals is distracting, noisy, confusing, stress-producing data smog is to these smog-analyzing machines a powerful new blueprint of human culture. "Our smallest actions leave digital trails," writes Nicholas Negroponte in *Wired.* "Blockbuster, American Express, and your local telephone company can suddenly pool their bits in a few keystrokes and learn a great deal about you. This is just the beginning: each credit-card charge, each supermarket checkout, and each postal delivery can be added to the equation."

The Tenth Law of Data Smog
Equifax is watching.

Information gathering has become so convenient and cost-effective that personal privacy has replaced censorship as our primary civil liberties concern. Dataveillance marks the transformation of meddlesome data smog into corporate rocket fuel. "Marketers should take full advantage of the information explosion to target specific individuals by economic, demographic, and lifestyle characteristics," exhorts a National Information Systems brochure boasting of a database with detailed information on 80 million consumers.

This unprecedented power of scrutiny is achieved without having to break the law or draw attention to the process. In fact, dataveillance is heavily reliant on quietude and probably would not survive prolonged public scrutiny. In January 1991, a shock wave reverberated through the marketing industry as American consumers openly revolted against a CD-ROM called Lotus MarketPlace. The database was to feature detailed personal information on 120 million American consumers in 80 million households, information collected by the leading credit reporting agency, Equifax. The portable, user-friendly CD-ROM was aimed at small businesses interested in customizing their own mailing lists from a vast, sortable registry of names, addresses, incomes, and buying habits.

But Americans loudly said *no.* They were not going to put up with that level of intrusion. In a short period of time, no fewer than 30,000 people phoned, faxed, and e-mailed messages to the software company Lotus, demanding that their names be removed from the database. Lotus and Equifax backed down; the CD-ROM was scrapped. The event was portrayed in the news media as a clear victory for consumer interests.

The triumph, however, was a mirage. In fact, every single scrap of data featured in Lotus MarketPlace was already publicly available and regularly being drawn on for marketing purposes—and still is. "In the great scheme of things," acknowledges privacy expert Mary Culnan, "[MarketPlace] was pretty benign stuff." The CD-ROM's demise, then, was no big win for consumers or privacy advocates. If anything, the liquidation of Lotus MarketPlace was a boost for big business over small business. Priced very cheaply at $695, the CD-ROM would have made the information much more affordable than it currently is as a closely held commodity leased out at exorbitant prices. Without realizing it, the MarketPlace consumer protesters were giving a lift to their chief enemies in the privacy wars: *Fortune* 500 companies. After the MarketPlace implosion, the rest of the industry let out an audible sigh of relief that the consumer revolt had barely even scratched their surface, and other companies quickly took steps to improve public relations and operate more quietly.

Sadly, the battle MarketPlace protesters believed they were fighting on behalf of all consumers was lost years ago, most definitively in 1974, when the Federal Privacy Act imposed severe restrictions on the government collection of personal data, but *exempted* business from any such constraints. Since that time, information technology has helped many companies to cultivate a massive collection of detailed personal data—height, weight, address, Social Security number, state of health, income, banking information, political affiliation, car model, price paid for home, contests entered into, magazine subscriptions, and so on—and to convert the sea of data into extremely useful information.

Lotus's major mistake, then, was to let its product become too visible, to let it look too much like Big Brother. This made it an easy scapegoat for mounting resentment against the loss of privacy (by 1990, 75 percent of Americans surveyed felt they had lost control over their personal information; this was up more than 25 percent from 1970). With a catchy name, a single recognizable product, and a familiar company moniker, MarketPlace quickly became *the* symbol of the increasing intrusion into consumer's private lives.

MarketPlace notwithstanding, times for the dataveillance industry have never been better. As long as the laws permit such sweeping information collection, technology is likely to work in the favor of dataveillance professionals. In *Snow Crash,* Neal Stephenson's apocalyptic cyber-thriller novel, the protagonists are introduced to the ancient Sumerian art of *neurolinguistic hacking*—tapping into a person's brainwaves and altering his or her thought process. Just as a computer hacker breaks through password barriers in order to gain access to sensitive files, a talented neurohacker can "go past all your defenses and sink right into your brainstem [and] exert absolute control" over your consciousness. The book's ruthless antagonist, media baron L. Bob Rife, has mastered neurohacking and is using it to slowly enslave people in his quest for world domination. A core troupe of Rife's victims are so beholden to him that they literally wear antennae on their heads so as to receive orders directly into their subconscious.

Anecdotes from the corridors of modern dataveillance come uncomfortably close to Stephenson's dark imagination. Twenty minutes ago, Jake Lamb was shopping for some jewelry for his wife's birthday in a Princeton, New Jersey, shopping mall, when two friendly men with clipboards approached him and asked if they could rent a half-hour of his time for fifty dollars. Now he sits in a darkened room and watches a wall as pages of *Playboy* magazine are projected onto it. Jake looks at each page exactly as long as he wishes, and then presses a button to go on to the next. That's all he has to do—a machine does the rest. While Jake looks at cigarette ads and women's breasts, a laser beam tracks the precise movement of his eyes and records exactly where they rest on each page and for how long. When he flips the last page, the lights are turned on and he walks back to the jewelry counter with a $50 bill in his pocket.

Back in the room, the lights go off again. Now, executives from Perception Research Services watch the same pages on the wall. But this time, the pages flip to Jake Lamb's exact tempo, and the laser is aimed the other way, producing a bright red dot precisely where Jake's eyes focused from moment to moment. On behalf of *Playboy*'s publisher and its advertisers, Perception Research Services has just rented a man's consciousness, roaming around in his brain and recording a replica of his second-to-second observations.

A few miles north, in Manhattan, Dr. Sidney Weinstein, a professor at New York University and president of Neuro Communication Research Laboratories, is using a different method to pursue the same prize. Weinstein clips sensors to his subjects' scalps and monitors their brainwaves while they watch a variety of advertisements. His analysis will show not only each subject's interest from second to second, but also which section of the brain is being aroused.

Perception Research and Neuro Communication are two cogs in a vast marketing research industry dedicated to uncovering the workings of the human brain. Millions of consumers like Jake Lamb are scrutinized every year for clues. "The answers they give," writes ad expert Eric Clark, "continuously swell the mass of data available to the marketing and advertising men. . . . The works of psychiatrists, psychologists, anthropologists, sociologists are raised and their theories adapted. Computers are used to collate and cross reference a mass of sometimes seemingly disparate information making it possible, for example, to find common links between people who buy dehydrated cooking sauce and pot plants."

Advanced technology helps this research progress every year, as modems automatically correlate incoming phone numbers to detailed consumer dossiers; electronic maps reveal incomes and rents for specific city blocks; CD-ROMs reveal the party affiliation and specific campaign donations of registered voters; health information companies monitor drugstore visits and funnel the information to doctors; and credit bureaus keep lengthy files on nearly every person's debt history. The torrent of data is collected by information processing companies like Claritas and Information Resources, Inc., and assembled into complex geodemographic and "psychographic" analyses, with the ultimate intent of mapping out a United States of Consumerism. "It's a whole new dimension for us," Young & Rubicam's Joseph Plummer told the *Atlantic Monthly* in 1984. "Before [psychographics], we didn't really have a sense of who the consumer out there was. Now we know how they live and what they buy—and why they buy it."

After another decade of honing the technology and the methodology, the psychographic consumer grail is said to be nearly within reach. Information Resources has a system under development called BehaviorScan, which aims to divine a comprehensive science of consumption by carefully plotting the correlation between external stimuli and the human urge to buy. Just as the name BehaviorScan eerily resembles "neurolinguistic hacking," marketing has become at least as terrifying as science fiction. A company called DejaNews Partners, for example, is copying and cataloguing, for marketing purposes, every single message posted onto every single Usenet newsgroup. Any business interested in locating people with a demonstrated interest in, say, fishing or gardening, will have names, e-mail addresses, and profile information written by the prospective customers themselves.

Another company, Educational Testing Service (ETS administrates the infamous SAT, LSAT, and GRE scholastic tests), is creating a nationwide database of high school attendance and grades against which potential employers soon will be able to run background checks.

Having cracked the code of consumer brains, the wild rumpus starts. Nazi propagandist Joseph Goebbels once said that given a sufficient "psychological understanding of the people concerned," it would not be an impossible task to convince a mass of people that a square is actually a circle. Dataveillance offers exactly such an understanding to thousands of ambitious corporations and political candidates. These exhaustive lists become much more than mere lists; they act as electronic psychoanalysts, sifting through billions of pieces of information to determine how and why people behave.

With elaborate consumer profiles on record, consumers come to resemble predictable machines themselves, ready and willing to respond affirmatively when just the right psychological button is pushed. "It's very well known that people are much more susceptible to persuasive appeals when they're distracted," explains University of Texas psychologist Dan Gilbert. "If I'm an advertiser, I want you to be under information load in as many circumstances as possible."

To understand why, it's helpful to revisit a historic and important philosophical dispute between seventeenth-century philosophers René Descartes and Baruch Spinoza. The debate was over how people perceive, and at what precise juncture a person decides whether or not to accept or reject a proposition. Put simply,

Descartes suggested that first we comprehend a notion, and then we either accept or reject. In slow motion, the Descartes paradigm looks like this:

CLAIM: "Look at my eyes. They're blue."
REACTION: *Okay, I understand your claim. Now, I will either agree or disagree. From the look of it, your eyes are brown, not blue. So I reject your claim.*

In contrast, Spinoza suggested that first we *simultaneously* comprehend *and accept* a notion, and only afterward, if we have time, are we able to *unaccept* it—that is, reject it. Spinoza implied that the rejection of a notion is a secondary psychological act. Spinoza in slow-mo:

CLAIM: "Look at my eyes. They're blue."
REACTION: *Okay, I understand and tentatively accept your claim as true. Now, I will consider whether or not I should change my acceptance to a rejection. Thinking about your claim for a split second, and noticing your eyes are brown, I find your claim preposterous. I reject your claim.*

Though Spinoza's argument is not as intuitive as Descartes's, intensive psychological testing has proven Spinoza to be correct. This finding is of critical importance in the context of the information glut, because under conditions of cognitive overload we rarely have the time or the focus to go back and question our initial acceptance of things. "We tend to make very unsophisticated inferences when we're under cognitive load," says Gilbert. "Thinking deeply cannot be done when you're loaded. Under cognitive load, a person can make a dispositional inference about somebody—*she's nice* or *she's kind* or *he's pro-choice.* But to take into account the other person's role in the situation, and how his role might be affecting his behavior—that's something that disappears as soon as someone becomes cognitively loaded."

The implications of this are extraordinary. If claims are more likely to be believed in an environment of information glut, consumers are almost certain to be increasingly vulnerable to commercial and political solicitations. Since today's glutted environment renders these same consumers distracted and easily open to the suggestions of these hyper-informed marketers, data smog may just be the best thing to come along for marketers since planned obsolescence.

chapter 14

Anecdotage

And so it was written and so it is said that many years ago the great Duwamish Indian Chief Seattle, ruler of six tribes around Puget Sound, became so disgusted by the rapacious behavior of the white race that he sat down and wrote an impassioned letter to the white president, Franklin Pierce. "The earth is our mother," he avowed. "I have seen a thousand rotting buffaloes on the prairies left by the white man who shot them from a passing train." Chief Seattle prodded President Pierce to examine the consequences of his people's actions: "What will happen when the buffalo are all slaughtered? The wild horses tamed? What will happen when the secret corners of the forest are heavy with the scent of many men and the view of the ripe hills is blotted by talking wires?"

So it is said, and so it is repeated: Not surprisingly, Chief Seattle's eloquent letter has become a pivotal document in the modern environmental movement, excerpted in fund-raising dispatches and read passionately at public demonstrations. Who can fail to be moved by such a noble and tragic petition? The letter invokes a collective social guilt for over a century of ethnic and environmental desecration.

But the document is not authentic. It was written by Texas screenwriter Ted Perry for a 1971 film on ecology. ("I wrote a speech which was fiction," Perry has acknowledged.) In real life, Chief Seattle was a fierce warrior, noted for his attacks on other Indian tribes. While he was purported to be a master statesman, he surely never laid eyes on a bison or a locomotive; nor could he have heard the chirp of a "whippoorwill," as Perry's letter also states. None of these three items were to be found within hundreds of miles of Chief Seattle while he was alive.

We can separate fact from fiction here in this book, just as it has been done in *The New York Times* and in other venues. We can repeat the facts over and over again, like some kind of mantra. But we cannot defeat the power of a good story, which explains why this fictional account of Chief Seattle, Ted Perry's version, has appeared on the "nonfiction" *New York Times* bestseller book list and has become a central part of Earth Day and other environmental celebrations in recent years. (The book is called *Brother Eagle, Sister Sky: A Message from Chief Seattle.*) "It's a classic case of a lie going twenty miles an hour when truth is just putting on its boots," says historian David Buerge.

Only now lies are even swifter. In the electronic age, a good lie well-told can zip around the world and back in a matter of seconds while the truth is trapped, buried under a filing cabinet full of statistics. While our fact-based society has largely overcome a past riddled with destructive myths and superstitions (we now know that disease is caused by microbes, rather than jealous gods, and that volcanic eruptions have nothing to do with virginity), one of the unwelcome consequences of information superabundance is that, in our increasingly distracting environment, we are more susceptible to simplifying, misleading myths.

The Eleventh Law of Data Smog

Beware stories that dissolve all complexity.

"The anecdote—selective, exaggerated, or just wrong, as a way of simplifying complicated issues—is back with a vengeance," says National Public Radio political analyst Daniel Schorr. "True, half-true, or untrue, horror stories seem to be the stuff of revolution in the media age."

If information glut can be likened to the danger of eating too much, *anecdotage* (a term coined by columnist William Safire) is like scarfing down too many sweets: It is a short-cut to quick pleasure and short-term satisfaction, but ultimately it can be unfulfilling and even dangerous—"empty calories" that can disturb a nutritious regimen. While we have recently been celebrating the power of myth with Joseph Campbell, Bill Moyers, and Robert Bly, we must also remember to fear it.

The double-edged quality is palpable. "Without metaphor, thought is inert," explains literacy scholar Frank Smith, likening the power of metaphor to a road map. People are instinctively able to draw inspiration and guidance from simple yet powerful stories—narratives—around which dry information coalesces and begins to make sense.

But what happens when these road maps for the mind feature roads and rivers that do not exist? Perhaps the most famous contemporary abuse of the anecdote was by Ronald Reagan, the "Great Communicator," who, in the presidential campaigns of 1976 and 1980, railed against a mythical "welfare queen" (never publicly named by Reagan), who had allegedly used eighty aliases, thirty addresses, twelve social security cards, and four nonexistent dead husbands to fraudulently collect $150,000. In fact, the closest actual case was a woman in Chicago who had used two false names to improperly collect $8,000. But Reagan's story stuck in the public imagination, not only helping him get elected president in 1980 but also propping up draconian welfare reform legislation in 1981. ("This particular initiative is disgusting," editorialized *The Washington Post* at the time. "We suppose that if you persist in viewing all welfare recipients as variations on the spectacular cheaters and 'welfare queens' who are periodically uncovered, it makes sense. But if you believe that welfare recipients are something other than a class of criminals and subhumans who need to be punished . . . then you will see this punitive, degrading act for what it is.")

Similarly, in September 1989, in a nationally televised speech from the Oval Office, George Bush displayed a bag of crack cocaine that he said had been seized in Lafayette Park, across the street from the White House; it did not matter that the bust had been staged specifically for his speech, and that crack is not regularly sold in Lafayette Park. The anecdote worked. It prompted a terrifying image of thugs dealing drugs in front of the "people's house."

We need not feel foolish for being so easily duped. We are born ready victims; our affinity for myth and metaphor comes hardwired into our brainstems. For most of our natural history, explains psychologist Richard Nisbett, "vivid information" has been the only way to learn. "I'd put it in evolutionary terms," he explains. "We're accustomed to the use of narrative information. That's the way we learned things in our previous, preliterate cultures. It's a relatively recent thing to learn about the world by statistics and by logical argument."

To document our reliance on narrative, Nisbett has conducted experiments in which subjects are presented with statistical data that conflicts with a narrative. In these experiments, the narrative always ends up making the dominant impression. In one such test, subjects were introduced to a prison guard who was either a reasonable, decent seeming fellow, or a brutal, bloodthirsty type. Then subjects were presented with hard data about what most prison guards are actually like, and were told to discount the impression they had from their encounter with the token guard. "It turns out," says Nisbett, "that being told that the guy you were seeing is *atypical* has absolutely no effect whatsoever on the inferences you make about prison guards in general. It doesn't matter. The only thing that matters is whether we show them a nice guy or a nasty guy. If we show them a nice guy, they think prison guards aren't so bad. If we show them a nasty guy, they think prison guards are really horrible."

A second experiment using welfare as the subject followed the same pattern with exactly the same results. "We show people a welfare case horror—a woman in her fourth generation of welfare, and we preface it by saying, 'Most people on welfare are there on a temporary basis, but we'd like you to read about an atypical case.' But it doesn't make a bit of difference whether we say it's typical or atypical. They make their judgments on welfare based on the people they've seen."

Psychologists confirm Daniel Schorr's hunch that anecdotage is a particular problem in the context of today's media age. "With the sophisticated mental apparatus we have used to build world eminence as a species," Robert Cialdini says of this catch–22, "we have created an environment so complex, fast-paced, and information-laden that we must increasingly deal with it in the fashion of the animals we long ago transcended." In this way, our information mania has sparked a behavioral *devolution*.

Journalists, the first line of defense against public deception, regularly fall prey to the power of misleading anecdotes, stories that compellingly fit their preconceived notions or suspicions about people or events. The danger now is that, in their increasing distraction, they too may be falling for them more than ever. Consider several lively political anecdotes of late.

Exhibit A: During the last year of his presidency, on a visit to a local supermarket, George Bush was reported to be baffled by a laser-guided grocery checkout scanner. "Bush Encounters the Supermarket, Amazed," ran *The New York Times* headline. Bush, who had been ensconced in the White House and the vice-presidential mansion for a total of eleven consecutive years, was thought to have become somewhat out of touch with the common person. Previously, a news story had appeared about how Bush had been unable to figure out a new-fangled gas pump at a gas station. The scanner story was just the confirmation journalists and Bush-skeptics were looking for. They lapped it up.

Though the anecdote got wide play, it turned out to be completely false. A *New York Times* reporter who hadn't even been on the scene had trumped up a much less interesting incident in which the manufacturer of a new-technology scanner was demonstrating its latest wares to Bush. But by the time the truth was discovered and reported, the severe damage to Bush's image was done. "It hurt the president badly in terms of public perception," writes Bush's press secretary Marlin Fitzwater. He went on to lose the election, largely because he was seen as out of touch with ordinary Americans.

Exhibit B: Headlines and newscasts blared one evening that President Clinton had prevented commuter flights at the Los Angeles Airport from taking off so that renowned Hollywood hairstylist Christophe could give him a leisurely coif on Air Force One. Again, the story also turned out to be false—one *unscheduled* flight was delayed for two minutes. But again the correction came too late. The original story struck a deep chord with the press and the American people, apparently confirming a suspicion that, now that he was in office, Clinton was also quickly losing his concern for the plight of the common folk. He quite literally wasn't concerned with keeping the trains or planes running on time. His approval ratings took a severe hit.

Exhibit C: In 1989 Rudolph Giuliani ran for Mayor of New York City and lost. On election night, as Giuliani began to deliver an extremely gracious concession speech in a ballroom filled with his supporters, a number of people in the audience loudly booed at the mention of the winning candidate, David Dinkins. Giuliani was understandably annoyed at this and attempted to get people to be quiet. "Quiet," he implored the crowd several times.

The next day, it was reported that Giuliani had rudely yelled "Shut up!" at his supporters. Though this actually never happened, the anecdote supported the widespread perception that Giuliani was too aggressive and mean-spirited to be an effective mayor; he wasn't genteel enough for the job. Giuliani was forced to apologize for the "shut up" remark, and it dogged him for years, even through his successful rematch campaign against Dinkins four years later.

Years after the alleged incident, after the "shut up" had become a part of New York political lore, a reporter from *The New York Times* happened to be reviewing a videotape of Giuliani's 1989 concession speech. The headline that ran in the *Times* the next day: "Famous Line was 'Quiet.' Not 'Shut Up.'"

Anecdotage is such an integral part of our culture, we even have a popular name for important narratives that probably aren't based in fact. We call such stories *apocryphal*.

APOCRYPHAL \ə-'päk-rə-fəl\ *adj*. 1. Of questionable authorship or authenticity. 2. Erroneous; fictitious.

Apocryphal. We grin as we let the word roll off our tongues with a decadent pleasure, sharing an invisible wink with anyone within earshot, saying, implicitly, *it's probably a lie—but then so much is these days.* This social norm bleeds into the work we do. In both business and politics, we constantly measure our success by the degree to which we are able to manipulate people's impressions through anecdotes.

Often, this gets carried to absurd ends, as when two account executives from the J. Walter Thompson advertising agency boasted in the *International Journal of Advertising* that a campaign exaggerating the uniqueness of a particular pain reliever had actually had a medical effect on customers. "Double-Blind trials demonstrated that branding accounts for a quarter to a third of the pain relief," they wrote. "Branding works like an ingredient of its own, interacting with the pharmacological active ingredients to produce something more powerful than the unbranded tablet."

The hubris in this claim is remarkable. Advertisers are not only proudly laying claim to having a medicinal effect with their commercials, but also justifying their own exaggerated claims about the pain reliever by saying that the exaggerations themselves are therapeutic. The message of this claim is that, since branding has been proven to reduce pain, we need not be concerned about any distortion of the truth along the way. Of course, apocrypha and consumer fraud have been around for ages. But the danger is that in our increasing distraction and speediness, the lies will move so much faster than the truth, they will too often become the truth.

chapter 15

The End of Journalism?

Public relations in the age of perpetual novelty

Upgrade mania, niche marketing, dataveillance, and anecdotage constitute an intimidating arsenal of marketing tools for tomorrow's salesperson. But perhaps the best news of all for marketers is that they increasingly have a direct line to their customers, unobstructed by the news media. "Tomorrow's communications techniques may allow PR people to bypass reporters completely," gushes a public relations newsletter. "Eliminating the media 'middlemen' also holds the potential of reducing the power of the press and forging more intimate bonds between PR people and their clients."

The Twelfth Law of Data Smog

On the information highway, most roads bypass journalists.

Reducing the power of the press is a terrible thing to do to a democratic society, but an enormous short-term value for anyone trying to sell something. For the business community and for politicians, the prospect of bypassing journalists holds the allure of circumventing public skepticism, intellectual curiosity, and rational analysis. It is the promise of being able to make an elaborate sales pitch completely uncontested. Conservative Republicans, for example, have already established two cable television networks, GOP-TV and National Empowerment Television (NET), funded by the conservative Free Congress Foundation. NET broadcasts programs produced by the National Rifle Association and the American Life League, an antiabortion group. "Though these programs can look like Discovery Channel documentaries," reports the *Columbia Journalism Review*, "they are in fact unrestrained, unfiltered, political infomercials."

"Infomercial" and "advertorial" are the two hybrid buzzwords of the emerging public relations bonanza. They refer to advertisements disguised to look like journalism, with the intent of eliciting from the consumer the kind of trust he or she would normally place in a newspaper article or TV news segment. One standard advertorial has a television news anchor–type person giving a quick, rosy summary of several movies just coming out from the same movie studio. Others are entire publications made to look like they are run by real journalists. A number of new investment magazines like *MoneyWorld*, *RealMoney*, and *Opportunist*, for example, come with a range of experts' suggestions for sound investments—all of whom, not coincidentally, are investors in the magazine. Can a consumer tell the difference between the bogus *MoneyWorld* and *RealMoney* and the bona fide *Money* and *Smart Money*? Sure, if she reads the fine print.

Real magazines also play the advertorial game by helping sponsors create ads that look like editorial content, as *Vogue* did recently in an eight-page advertorial for Lee Riveted Jeans. ("We saw this as a hugely added value," said David Smith, manager of consumer advertising for Lee.)

Websites also specialize in blurry crossover between advertising and editorial content. But perhaps the most insidious info-mercials/advertorials today can be found in the school classroom, where marketing companies like Lifetime Learning Systems peddle specially designed ad packages that look like real educational materials. "Kids spend 40 percent of each day in the classroom, where traditional advertising can't reach them," Lifetime explains in promotional literature to potential clients. "Now you can enter the classroom through custom-made learning materials created with your specific marketing objectives in mind. Communicate with young spenders directly and, through them, their teachers and families as well." Students have learned the value of clear-cutting from Procter & Gamble and the lumber company Georgia Pacific; they have been taught about important inventors Gregor Mendel, Louis Pasteur, George Washington Carver, and Orville Redenbacher; and they have been taught about the benefits of nuclear power courtesy of the American Nuclear Society.

Concurrent with the rise in advertorials, there has been a steady decline in viewership of television news, particularly among adults under thirty, as well as a striking erosion of newspaper readership. As niche media proliferates and consumers get their news from a wider variety of sources, media entrepreneurs can even begin to plausibly suggest that journalists have become obsolete. "Why should the media be allowed to filter your message anyway?" demands America Online services president Ted Leonsis. "In the near future, everybody will have access to all the information they need to make their own decisions. So who needs the media to deliver content? I hate to say it, but I think the media are in a death spiral."

Who needs the news media? Given the low opinion of the fourth estate, and its declining audience, Leonsis's blunt question must be taken at face value. What is the value of having a news media, circa 1997? When Adolph Ochs purchased *The New York Times* in 1896, he declared "news" a vital public service and promised to "give the news, all the news . . . and give it as early, if not earlier, than can be learned through any other reliable medium." But something happened on the way to Ochs's vision of journalistic excellence: Information came into abundance. First radio and then television put news consumers directly on the scene; now the Internet has turned ordinary citizens into reporters, publishers, and broadcasters. For example: My local paper didn't arrive on my doorstep this morning, so I checked the New York City weather forecast on the National Weather Service Web page. As Leonsis correctly asserts, the new media increasingly allows people to find much of the information they need without having to consult traditional journalists.

But journalism is not limited to "news," and Leonsis's declaration foolishly overlooks the larger value of journalism, which is not made obsolete by the emerging capability of consumers to directly locating pertinent information. Journalists help explain our own lives and society to us. If not journalists, who else will expose medical frauds and careless doctors? Who else will hold politicians to their promises? Who else will examine the design, intent, and honesty of advertising? Who else will monitor the link between campaign contributions and political favors? Who else will monitor airline, train, and automobile safety?

For the sake of society, journalism must prevail over advertorials. Businesses interested in sales are not always interested in what consumers would consider the whole truth. Politicians interested in votes have the same type of motivation. For this simple reason, we all desperately need journalists. The journalist's loyalty is to some semblance of fairness, if not pure objectivity, whereas the loyalty of marketers is to sales of a particular product.

In fact, journalists are *more* necessary in the glutted world. As a skeptical analytical buffer and—now more than ever—as an arbiter of statistical claims, the news media is an indispensable public utility, every bit as vital as our electricity and gas lines. In a world with vastly more information than it can process, journalists are the most important processors we have. They help us filter information without spinning it in the direction of one company or another. Further, as society becomes splintered, it is journalists who provide the vital social glue to keep us at least partly intact as a common unit. For democracy as we know it, a bypassed media would be a disaster.

PR is not, however, the biggest threat to journalism in the information age. *Information* is. As journalists fend off attacks from public relations aggressors and new media entrepreneurs, they're also going to have to take care not to invite their own extinction by giving into the temptations of perpetual novelty.

Since the dawn of civilization, humans have been constructing a quilt of community understanding out of new information, gathered and passed around. In a world of information scarcity, messenger/journalists performed the vital community service of acquiring and transmitting fresh data. "[Newspapers are] that universal circulation of intelligence," wrote Arthur Young in 1793, "which in England transmits the last vibration of feeling or alarm, with electric sensibility, from one end of the Kingdom to another." Before information became a plentiful resource, nuggets of new information served as valuable currency. Journalists in the pre-electronic era acted as hunter–gatherers, foraging for virtually anything they could find.

As information has come into super-abundance over the past fifty years, however, this hunter–gatherer role has been rendered partially obsolete. People have become their own publishers and broadcasters, and new information has become relatively easy to come by. In fact, a formidable instant-news industry has emerged in the form of CNN, CNN*fn,* MSNBC, and assorted other all-news networks, channels, and news wires, to feed us news tidbits all day and all night long.

But the news-flash industry supplies us with entertainment, not journalism, and as such is part of the problem of information glut. While most of the subjects mentioned in hourly news updates are of great national or international importance, the actual news nuggets being reported are of little or no practical or intellectual value. The

Dow Jones Industrial Average is up thirteen and a half points at this hour; the space shuttle's launch was scrapped due to bad weather; the jury in the O. J. Simpson trial has been selected; President Clinton declared that the Bosnian elections should go forward. These are not by any means trivial subjects, but they contain zero educational worth when covered in news-nugget fashion. Our fundamental understanding of Bosnia or the stock market is not going to change, no matter how many news-bites we hear about them. To actually learn about the subject requires not a series of updates, but a careful and thoughtful review of the situation. One long newspaper or magazine article, which would take up no more time than twenty one-minute news nuggets, would do it.

News bites continue not because they are valuable, but because they are dramatic and entertaining—and because, in an age of very little common information, they give us all some small nugget of common information to grasp onto for a few hours. They give people a false sense of connectedness and understanding, and make us feel informed when we really aren't. As such, we would be much better off ignoring the vast majority of them.

News is not, of course, completely irrelevant; we will always need to stay abreast of local, national, and world affairs. But the value of hourly and daily updates will pale in comparison to information we already have on hand—how to feed and clothe ourselves, fight pestilence, and govern ourselves. The new challenge is to share this information with one another, to manage it thoughtfully, and to transform it into knowledge inside billions of individual brains. This is not so much fact hunting as it is data gardening.

Unfortunately, many journalists reflexively balk at the prospect of sharing "old" information, at stories that smell of "old news" ("We've covered that" . . . "It's been done"). Instead, reporters report whatever feels newest: the latest opinion poll, today's shocking personal indiscretion, this morning's testimony. "My job is not to educate the public," insists television producer Steve Friedman. "My job is to tell the public what's going on."

Friedman's distinction is critical. *Education* assumes a responsibility for making sure that knowledge sticks, while mere *telling* focuses on the mechanics of transmitting the most compelling information of the moment. By limiting their purview to mere news flashes, journalists are absolving themselves of any over-arching obligation to the audience. They are freed from having to consider the information variant of the tree-falls-in-the-woods dilemma: *If information gets reported, but everyone is too distracted to notice it and it therefore falls on deaf ears, was it adequately reported?*

The question of whether the news-flash mindset is obsolete came up among a group of producers in a weekly editorial meeting I attended years ago for National Public Radio's *Talk of the Nation.* One of us had suggested an educational show on AIDS prevention, in light of polls that showed much ignorance on the subject. But both the senior producer and the host quashed the idea, on the grounds that it was out of journalistic bounds. *This information has already been reported,* they insisted. *It is not our job to report old news.*

Incidents like this illustrate that journalists are stubbornly refusing to adapt to a new paradigm of sharing information. The traditional news media hasn't yet come to terms with the fundamental paradigm shift from scarcity to glut, which is why Yahoo, Alta Vista, Excite, and the other World Wide Web libraries are on their way to becoming our primary information sources. In our increasingly asynchronous environment, consumers are eagerly demonstrating that the feeling is mutual. They are turning their attention away from news flashes and toward unabashed educators who aren't afraid of "old news." In doing so, they recognize that the information glut cannot be ignored, but it can be nurtured into one heck of a productive garden.

To appreciate the scope of the transition journalism must now undergo, it might be helpful to look at the history of one news service, *Editorial Research Reports,* which is published out of Washington, D.C., by Congressional Quarterly. *Reports* was created in the 1920s as an information service for journalists—specifically for newspaper editorial writers who were long on opinions but short on actual data. "In the '20s and '30s," says Marcus Rosenbaum, a former editor of the service, "they didn't have many sources to find out information. They had the news wires, the library, and their clip files. They also had an encyclopedia and their own general knowledge from school. This was the case even in the '60s and '70s.

"But by the time I got there in the late '80s, the problem was a different one. Our clients now had sources for any kind of information they wanted. They could do reporting online; they could go to databases like NEXIS and Data Times; they could pick up the phone and call people. So our new job, instead of throwing lots of information at them, was to distill lots of information into something that they could read. If you do a NEXIS search on welfare reform, you're going to have 53,000 hits. What do you do with that? But if I can give it to you in 8,000 words, that will be interesting."

Rosenbaum is describing the paramount challenge of the modern journalist: to be the tenders of electronic archives of all human knowledge, more like proactive electronic librarians than newsflashers. Such a world necessitates a restructured value system in which sharing and summarizing existing information is more of a priority than is stumbling onto genuinely new data. The new-news/old-news paradigm has become outmoded. New information for its own sake is no longer a goal worthy of our best reporters, our best analysts, our best minds. Journalists will need to take a more holistic approach to information as a natural resource that has to be *managed* more than *acquired*.

What we need is not so much *news* but shared understanding. Who has relevant information, and who needs it? We must learn to share information with one another, to manage it thoughtfully, and to transform it into universal knowledge. The present-day *New York Times* has acknowledged this to a certain degree, as have the newsweeklies, slowly remaking their products as not so much news services but rather as hubs for important *news analysis*. They do this as a recognition that much of the freshest news is now transmitted via television and the Internet. Print is now in the eternal position of lagging behind.

A more fundamental reorientation in response to the information glut can be seen in recent journalistic success stories like *The Utne Reader,* a bimonthly magazine that bills itself as "The Best of the Alternative Media." *Utne* culls stories from hundreds of different journals across the country, reprinting condensed versions of some and bundling others into thousand-word issue summaries. A typical *Utne* piece will sew together information and ideas obtained from four or more other stories. The more recently introduced *National Times* performs a service similar to *Utne,* but on a more "mainstream" political level. Many other newspapers like *The Washington Post* and magazines such as *The Nation* now feature regular "magazine reader" columns, in which a reporter sifts, *Utne*-like, through the media glut and pulls out a few especially worthy stories.

In addition, a growing number of journalists are joining an ambitious rethinking of journalism called "public journalism." These advocates argue for a radical shift toward shared, relevant information, and away from new information for the sake of being new. To the extent that they recognize the new information environment, public journalism and similar movements reevaluating the role of journalists are not merely sensible. They are utterly necessary.

chapter 16

Cyber-libertarians vs. Technorealists

One of Newt Gingrich's first acts after being sworn in as Speaker of the U.S. House of Representatives in January 1995 was to make all Congressional documents publicly available on the Internet, on a Website called Thomas (named after Thomas Jefferson). This singular deed, he declared, would "change the balance of power—because knowledge is power. If every citizen had the access to information that the Washington lobbyists have, we would have changed the balance of power in America towards the citizens and out of the Beltway."

He knows better, of course. Gingrich is smart enough to understand that opening the floodgates of information doesn't automatically turn Americans into better citizens. To the contrary, while some political specialists have benefited from the comprehensive

e, the average citizen has been more apt than before to get
flood. It's *focus* that brings knowledge and power, not dif-

grich is smiling broadly anyway, because the Internet
changes the balance of power toward *him*. One of the information
revolution's most outspoken proponents, Gingrich has for decades
been fervently talking up the virtues of microprocessors and modems for one simple reason: It furthers his own cause. "The information age," Gingrich has said, "means more decentralization, more
market orientation, more freedom for individuals, more opportunity for choice, more capacity to be productive without controls by
the state." Gingrich is absolutely correct. But it's important to remember that unbridled decentralization and market orientation
will also have some unwelcome consequences for all of us. In this
emerging electronic frontier, common discourse is no longer nurtured, and the notion of a government as a guarantor of public
health, safety, and welfare is seriously threatened.

The Thirteenth Law of Data Smog (Gingrich's Law)
Cyberspace breeds libertarianism.

Because cyberspace functions so well as a decentralized network,
it tends to foster a politics of ardent libertarianism. Many "neti-
zens," as *Wired* magazine calls Internet aficionados, advocate a society in which government interference is minimal, where individual
choice is virtually unrestrained. They are understandably inspired
to such thinking by the computing and networking technologies
that are so empowering. Other modern technologies also tend to
favor this shift in power, and inspire similar political leanings. In
fact, suggests writer Andrew Shapiro, if one scratches the surface of
both the information and biotech revolutions, what one discovers
right underneath is a "control revolution," a massive transfer of
power from bureaucracies to individuals and corporations. In an
unregulated control revolution, free markets and consumer choice
become even more dominant forces in society than they already are,

and in virtually every arena social regulation gives way to economic incentive. Rampant consumerism augments the ubiquitousness of pop culture and the free-for-all competition for scarce resources. Ultimately, even social intangibles like privacy become commodified.

This extrapolation from the digital to the political can catch even the most sophisticated analysts off-guard. In 1994 Esther Dyson, a leading cyber thinker, was invited to a conference to discuss her views on the Internet. Before she came, she was asked to help draft a document extolling the virtues of deregulation in cyberspace; only later did she discover that she had been co-opted into endorsing a broad libertarian manifesto.

That episode, along with a string of personal conversations with Gingrich, led Dyson to understand that she and the rest of the cyber elites (the "digerati") have been inadvertently assisting Gingrich's radical political agenda of "devolution." "He 'gets it,'" Dyson writes of Gingrich. "But what does he want to do with what he gets? Do I want to live in the world he wants to create?"

Here is one political revolution that will not only be televised; it also has a home page: http://www.pff.org. This Website, sponsored by the Progress & Freedom Foundation, a think tank closely associated with Gingrich,[*] is the virtual headquarters for cyber-libertarianism. PFF founders Jeff Eisenach and George Keyworth were among the earliest pols to shrewdly recognize the inherent nexus between information technology and libertarian values. Their manifesto, "Cyber-space and the American Dream: A Magna Carta for the Knowledge Age," declares that "Accelerating demassification creates the potential for vastly increased human freedom. It also spells the death of the central institutional paradigm of modern life, the bureaucratic organization. (Governments, including the American government, are the last great redoubt of bureaucratic

---

[*] So that contributions to PFF may be considered tax deductible under the 501(c)(3) designation of the Internal Revenue Service, the foundation claims to be both educational and nonpartisan. This is one of the most common abuses of the federal tax code.

power on the face of the planet, and for them the coming change will be profound and probably traumatic.)"

At PFF they live by a number of credos. The first is that we are at a pivotal point in American civilization, where the emerging information economy allows for a tremendous amount of economic and cultural progress. The second credo is a warning that the full advantages of the information revolution will not be realized unless and until the American people cooperate by supporting drastic cutbacks in government. "[The Knowledge Age] will not deliver on its potential," insists the Magna Carta, "unless it adds social and political dominance to its accelerating technological and economic strength. This means repealing Second Wave laws and retiring Second Wave attitudes." ("Second Wave" is a reference to Gingrich's mentor Alvin Toffler, whose doctrine of the Third Wave of civilization has been co-opted by cyber-libertarians. As summarized by Toffler, the First Wave was defined by thousands of years of agrarian-based culture; the Second Wave was what we have been calling the Industrial Age of the last few hundred years; the Third Wave is where material things become secondary to the transfer of information, a transition that began in the 1950s.)

Not coincidentally, the "Second Wave policies" that PFF wants so badly to do away with are the very same policies that conservative Republicans have been railing against for decades—federal government programs established in the New Deal and Great Society eras that enable government to ensure workplace fairness and safety, environmental health, and assistance for the poor and elderly. Though by and large these are policies that the American people have supported and continue to desire from government, the Republicans have brilliantly managed to cast many of them in an antiprogress light. There is another way to welcome technological progress into society, a course that does not require a radical political "devolution." A group of writers, of which I am a member, have been recently trying to articulate a more thoughtful avenue, which we call "technorealism."

Technorealism is an attempt at a more balanced response to the technological revolution, appreciating the benefits of technology while keeping a careful eye out for the drawbacks. Technorealism rejects the notion that cyberspace or any technology is a truly autonomous world unto itself, exempt from all laws and social conventions. Rather, there is an appropriate (if limited) role for government insuring that all new technologies serve the public interest. To quote from an overview of Technorealism (available on the Web at www.technorealism.org and reprinted in full on page 217):

> While governments should respect the rules and customs that have arisen in cyberspace, and should not stifle this new world with inefficient regulation or censorship, it is foolish to say that the public has no sovereignty over what an errant citizen or fraudulent corporation does online. As the representative of the people and the guardian of democratic values, the state has the right and responsibility to help integrate cyberspace and conventional society.
>
> Technology standards and privacy issues, for example, are too important to be entrusted to the marketplace alone. Competing software firms have little interest in preserving the open standards that are essential to a fully functioning interactive network. Markets encourage innovation, but they do not necessarily insure the public interest.

It will ultimately be up to the American people, of course, as to whether our society responds to technological innovation with a libertarian or technorealism disposition. I believe it is one of the most important decisions we will make as a nation in the next century.

PART. 4

A Return to Meaning

Superabundant information is grand,
until we understand that it can rob us of
the peace that is our spiritual birthright.
We have only recently realized our need
to develop an ecological relationship
with the natural world. Perhaps we
must also realize our need for inner
ecology, an ecology of mind.

—philosopher Philip Novak

chapter 17

What Then Must Be Done?

Data smog is a permanent new feature of our social landscape. It cannot be disposed of any more easily than toxic waste or obesity, and coming to grips with the consequences of speedy information is going to be a lot more challenging than simply identifying its consequences. As we begin to face the challenge, it is helpful first to reflect on how, in two recent instances, American society has confronted other costly overindulgences. In the late 1960s and early '70s, Americans began to realize that industrial smog and sludge accruing all around them wasn't just unsightly—it was also toxic. Around the same time, nutritionists started to boost awareness about the severe consequences of consuming too many calories and too much fat.

Now a similar challenge befalls citizens of the information age. For our own individual well-being and for the welfare of our democratic society, we must act now to responsibly limit our exposure to information. To return to the wisdom of Eli Noam: "Almost anybody can *add* information. The difficult question is how to *reduce* it."

The very idea of actively eliminating information is such anathema to our culture, it is enshrined as one of our few social taboos under the label of "censorship." Not only is it instinctively distasteful, on first blush wholesale reduction of information also seems like an impossible proposition, analogous to stopping sand from accruing on a beach. As Brian Lamb responded to Eli Noam at Columbia University that afternoon, "You can't stop this process. It's the American way. Which part of the library or the Internet do you want to shut down?"

But the problem is not as hopeless as Lamb suggests. Success on both the environmental and nutrition fronts over the last several decades did not come easily or quickly, but it did come.* Americans have risen to confront vexing challenges many times in the past after becoming sufficiently informed.

It is with this task of spreading awareness that we must begin. Almost a decade before the first Earth Day in 1970, Rachel Carson published *Silent Spring,* an exposé revealing the devastating consequences of pesticide manufacturing and use. The book became a runaway bestseller and sparked an entirely new way of popular thinking about our environment. In the public mind, conservation was elevated to the same level of importance as industrial "progress." Over time, it became reflexive thinking that the two forces had to be balanced in order to maintain the type of society we would want to continue living in.

Similarly, we must now strive to return to an equilibrium between the three basic elements of our information ecology—production, distribution, and processing. The goal should be to maintain and even increase ready access to reliable communication

---

* As Gregg Easterbrook points out in *A Moment on the Earth,* environmental regulations of the '70s and '80s were a dramatic success, comprising one of the great unheralded triumphs of modern government. This fact is not as widely acknowledged as it should be, says Easterbrook, because of two distinct conceits: Environmentalists depend on a crisis mentality to keep donations coming in, while conservative industrialists don't like to give the government credit for anything.

and useful information, but to do so without compromising a certain social serenity and without allowing society to disintegrate into a fragmented, fractious electronic tower of babel—its citizens not able to come together nor even understand one another.

To begin this process, let us first elevate our discussion of the implications of the information revolution far above the merits of the latest version of Netscape, the prospect of a $500 computer, and the impending IPOs of ISPs (initial public offerings of Internet service providers). Like industrialization and food abundance, ready information is undeniably a good thing. But there are also complex and disturbing "disservice effects" that warrant constant attention. Once we reach a critical mass of understanding on these issues, the stage will be set for actual antidotes to the problem, ranging from individual efforts to comprehensive government action. The good news is, there are a number of promising remedies for data smog. They are ours to invoke if we have the will to do so.

chapter 18

Be Your Own Filter

The first remedy is to identify the clutter and start sweeping it away. Most of us have excess stimuli and data in our lives, distracting us, pulling us away from our priorities and from a much-desired tranquility. If we stop just for a moment to look (and listen) around us, we will begin to notice a series of data streams that we'd be better off without, including some distractions we pay handsomely for.

Turn the television off. There is no quicker way to regain control of the pace of your life, the peace of your home, and the content of your thinking than to turn off the appliance that supplies for all-too-many of us the ambiance of our lives. Millions of Americans have been discovering the serenity and empowerment that comes with using the OFF switch, not to mention hours and hours of newly acquired free time with which they can begin to do some of the things they've never found time for in the past. For a few years, the organization TV-Free America has been leading a National TV-Turnoff Week every spring, inspiring people to venture into that strange place where sitcom and soap opera characters cannot go: real life.

It is not enough to simply turn the TV off; one must also make it somewhat difficult to turn it on again. Many TV-free participants have liked the results so much that they have gotten rid of their televisions altogether. My own alternative to this radical gesture has been to move the offending item from our kitchen/living room into the closet. There it stays except for a few select hours per week, when I lug it out, plug it in, and turn it on. After our brief viewing, it goes straight back to the closet. Making TV somewhat cumbersome to watch has made all the difference in our lives. Since we consigned our television to the closet, my wife and I play more music, we read more, we talk more.

Giving up the television, or even reducing the weekly allotment, isn't nearly as easy as it sounds. There is a reason we watch so much of it. Television is physically hypnotic, an extremely comfortable way to forget about our troubles and tensions in the real world. One key to its enormous success is that even stupid television is mesmerizing. The more channels we have to choose from, the greater the temptation to surf around from one unsatisfying offering to another.

A suggested trade-off: Cancel your cable TV service (we did this several years ago), and apply that same $20 per month to one or more good books. Books are the opposite of television: They are slow, engaging, inspiring, intellect-arousing, and creativity-spurring.

Avoid news-nuggets. All-news channels, wire services, and top-of-the-hour headlines may be the only fabric we have left holding us together as a nation, but that isn't reason enough to sacrifice your attention span to the incessant drone of traffic updates, murder trial play-by-play, postures of outrage from the president and the mayor, composites from the NYSE and NASDAQ, and a dozen sports scores you don't much care about. But we all pay attention anyway, because of the drama. An hour later, we will get an update on the new composite and the latest political soundbite. Now the Dow is down, now the mayor is blaming the labor union. Each day becomes a real-life soap opera, with news-bits so brief that it is nearly impossible to learn anything substantial.

Skip them. Spend those five minutes each hour doing something more productive, like conducting one meaningful conversation. To be a well-informed citizen, spend some quality time each day reading more thorough news and news analysis.

Leave the pager and cell-phone behind. It is thrilling to be in touch with the world at all times, but it's also draining and interfering. Are wireless communicators instruments of liberation, freeing people to be more mobile with their lives—or are they more like electronic leashes, keeping people more plugged-in to their work and their info-glutted lives than is necessary and healthy? For sanity's sake, people ought to be allowed to roam free away from the information superhighway for at least some portion of each week.

Limit your e-mail. As one spends more and more time online, e-mail quickly changes from being a stimulating novelty to a time-consuming burden, with dozens of messages to read and answer every day from colleagues, friends, family, newsgroup posts, and unsolicited sales pitches. The biggest problem with e-mail is also its greatest virtue: It's cheap. The transaction cost is so low in terms of both money and effort that people find it all too easy to transmit messages and contact you. Many electronic glutizens have picked up the very bad habit of forwarding every entertaining nugget they receive—jokes, urban myths, electronic chain letters, and more—to everyone on their electronic address book.

Recall the playful warning from MIT's Michael Dertouzos: "E-mail is an open duct into your central nervous system. It occupies the brain and reduces productivity." For those of us who spend a fair amount of time working on a computer, maintaining control over our e-mail in-boxes is critically important. If we're spending too much time each day reading and answering e-mail that has virtually no value, we must take steps to control it. Ask people (nicely) not to forward trivia indiscriminately. "Unsubscribe" to the newsgroups that you're no longer really interested in. Tell spammers that you have no interest in their product, and ask them to remove you from their customer list. (Specific instructions on how to reduce electronic spam appear in Appendix B.)

Say no to dataveillance. With some determination and a small amount of effort, one can also greatly reduce the amount of junk mail and unsolicited sales phone calls. It involves writing just a few letters, requesting to have your name put on "do-not-disturb" lists, which some 75 percent of direct marketers honor. (Specific instructions on how to get on these lists appear in Appendix B.)

Resist advertising. We read, watch, and listen to advertisements all day. Must we also wear them on our clothes?

Resist upgrade mania. Remember: Upgrades are designed to be sales tools, not to give customers what they've been clamoring for.

Be your own "smart agent." A new class of robotic "smart agent" software is becoming available to help consumers automate their information-filtering needs—software such as IBM's InfoSage, mentioned in chapter ten, which delivers a customized set of news stories according to programmed preferences. Other programs weed out e-mail not written by a select list of people.

But for reasons we've already discussed, smart agents are not the answer to the information glut. Regardless of how efficient they become, they will never be adequate substitutes for our own manual filtering. Instead, we must become our own smart agents.

As your own smart agent, you are responsible for managing your own personal signal-to-noise ratio, enhancing the signal—information that is accurate, relevant, economical, articulate, and evocative—and eliminating anything that blocks out or distracts meaning. At its most merciful, noise appears as annoyingly obvious nfjidnqiub and distinct zlpibiurfrh obstacles jdoieiijfqiworjois. More often, though, noise comes cleverly disguised as meaningful information, in the form of wordy, redundant sentences that drag on much too long, that could have said the same type of thing or delivered the same kind of message in fewer words and before you even know what is happening or has happened you've wasted time and effort reading or viewing a bloated stream of information that has distracted your sense of clarity and doesn't ever seem to end.

Ultimately, determining what qualifies as signal and what is merely noise is a subjective experience. Each individual must judge what is noise, and devise personal filtering mechanisms. But the person who does not even inquire—this is the person who will surely continue contributing to the smog and choking on it with the rest of us.

Cleanse your system with "data-fasts." As your own smart agent, you are also your own data dietitian. Take some time to examine your daily intake and consider whether or not your info diet needs some fine-tuning. Take some data naps in the afternoon, during which you stay away from electronic information for a prescribed period. You could also consider limiting yourself to no more than a certain number of hours on the Internet each week, or at least balancing the amount of time spent online with an equal amount of time reading books.

In addition to the daily regimen, many victims of glut (including Eamon Dolan, the data-saddled editor of this book) have found that periodic data fasts of a week or month have a remarkably rejuvenating effect. One sure way to gauge the value of something, after all, is to go without it for a while.

chapter 19

Be Your Own Editor

After learning how to filter input, one must shift concern to the equally important task of limiting output. Here, we also have a new creed to adopt, and a playful new slogan:

Give a hoot, don't info-pollute.

Introducing the concept of the information litterbug. Amidst the data smog, a new kind of social responsibility has emerged—an obligation to be succinct. Just as we've had to curtail our toxic emissions in the physical world, the information glut demands that we all be more economical about what we say, write, publish, broadcast, and post online. People who recklessly pump redundant or obfuscatory information into society are the information age equivalents of the miscreants who open their car door at a stop light to dump trash onto the street.

There's nothing inherently wrong with complexity or length, so long as it has a purpose. But try to avoid verbosity and the gratuitous use of images. Everything from voice-mail messages to office memos to book reports to speeches to Web pages should be crisp, clear, and to the point. This is our new obligation to one another. By reducing the amount of needless information, we will also reduce the amount of vulgarity, as people feel less need to be sensational to attract attention. Our tone will become more civil. Our social signal-to-noise ratio will begin to improve.

These efforts to counteract the information glut should be a natural extension of long-standing endeavors to stay humble, decent, modest. We who have learned not to drink or eat or work or rest to excess will now simply add another virtue to the list. Now we will also avoid information profligacy.

In order to live up to this new responsibility, it behooves us to search for tools to assist us. On a recent rummaging excursion through our Uncle Chuck's storage closets, my brother Jon, a film-maker, unearthed an old Super 8 movie camera. Unlike the eight-track tape players and various other gadgets that we've found over the years, this camera still works and the mechanics are not yet fully obsolete. One can still buy Super 8 film and pay to have it processed. But it is a dated technology, and Uncle Chuck, ever the family archivist, had long since replaced it with a series of more convenient and versatile video camcorders.

Jon was drawn to the camera because of the old-movie sensation one gets from watching Super 8 movies. The events on film, even if just recently shot, seem to have taken place in some distant past. This is because Super 8 runs at eighteen frames per second, while modern TV and videotape feature the equivalent of thirty frames per second. Also, Super 8 and all film movies have a brief moment of black—a flicker—between frames. The differences conspire to give the modern viewer the illusion that the filmed events happened at a slower speed. It is a vaguely comforting feeling, somehow imbuing the filmed action with some sort of mythic quality.

A much more profound limitation of Super 8 is that each roll of film lasts just three minutes. Compared to your standard VHS camcorder tape of two hours, that's a pretty burdensome restriction. Not much of the afternoon picnic is going to fit on a three-minute tape. Not much of a walk around the Grand Canyon. Not much of a family wedding. Also, while camcorder output is viewable as soon as it finishes rewinding, Super 8 requires a developing fee and weeks of processing time.

Super 8s were popular in their day, but they were never cheap or convenient enough to become a household staple. The camcorder, though, is everywhere. It has become an integral part of the American suburban family lifestyle. Home video archives have blossomed, filling shelves with scores of hours of toddlers learning to walk, swing, bike, swim, and so on. The tape is so long and inexpensive that camcorders are routinely brought out for family events and simply left running, so as not to miss anything. As today's colossal computer hard drives allow us to access and store a nearly unlimited amount of text, today's camcorders do the same with sound and images.

So why does it all turn out to be such a dreadful bore? Home video cameras are a major technological and populist breakthrough, on the level of the portable typewriter—bestowing on the masses an ability that for nearly a century belonged only to the rich and powerful. So how come the camcorder's most significant gift to world culture is *America's Funniest Home Videos*?

On the whole, we find camcorder material to be terrifically dull and lifeless. Ironically, the medium that technologically has *so* much feels like it is missing something important when we finally sit down to watch two full hours of little Eric spending the afternoon trying to escape training wheels. We never had that feeling while watching the infinitely more limited Super 8.

I experienced this unsettling paradox first-hand when I asked Jon to film my wedding. He owns a rather sophisticated Hi–8 camcorder, but he left that at home. Instead, he chose to shoot on Chuck's old Super 8. In five hours, he got through four rolls—twelve minutes—of film. Weeks went by while we waited for it to come back from the developers. Finally, we sat down to watch our measly twelve minutes of footage. It was over in a flash. But we were thrilled. That twelve chopped-up minutes of flickery, slow-motiony dances and party conversation seem so much more satisfying than the long, utterly comprehensive wedding videos I had seen in the past. We had gotten more with less.

The lesson of the camcorder is that the medium that captures almost everything conveys almost nothing. The three-minute Super 8 films of our wedding are cherished glimpses into that event, while an uninterrupted three-hour video of a wedding and reception dulls our senses and renders our memories useless. It overloads us. Like a meal where we eat far too much and feel sick, or a bathtub left running for too long, it smothers the original experience.

"The challenge I learned in film school," Jon says, "is how to edit the film so that it conveys its message in as short a time as possible. There was a creed in our department: Is that frame absolutely necessary?"

In the information society, this challenge applies to every one of us. Is that word/image absolutely necessary? Technology has given us the power to gather lifetimes of information and to broadcast the data at almost no effort or cost. With that opportunity comes the awesome responsibility of self-editing, of information restraint.

The good news is, the payoff for this restraint is high. As we severely limit content, we learn to savor it more. As an illustration of this point, pick up any collection of poetry. Or tune into Garrison Keillor's weekly public radio show, *A Prairie Home Companion*. Keillor is a modern hero of information restraint. He speaks slowly, never in a hurry to get anyplace, always savoring words and ideas and memories along the way. In his regular installments of "News from Lake Wobegon," he vividly conveys the emotional landscape of his fictional neighbors in just a few hundred spoken words, patiently doling out phrases one at a time, not moving forward until each one is etched into the listener's imagination. His stories are a sanctuary from the glutted life, a place where anyone can go to be touched by a few simple sounds, smells, and feelings. Along with many other works of art that employ brevity as a vehicle for meaning and understanding, they are paragons of virtue in our new information ecology.

chapter 20

Simplify

Between input and output, there is life itself. How does one live a meaningful life in an ever-more complex and distracting world? One helpful ingredient, I've found, is to embrace a new paradigm of simplicity.

Several years ago, I became interested in the extremely low-tech enterprise of pinhole photography, which many of us first encountered in grade school. With just a pin, a cardboard box, some tinfoil, some photographic paper, and a few trays of chemicals, I found I could capture interesting images and develop them in my basement immediately. While the images were not about to win any awards, they were meaningful to me. The entire process yielded a surprising amount of pride and satisfaction.

At the time, I could not articulate why I so preferred pinhole to the more advanced home photography methods, in which I had also dabbled. All I knew was that I found meaning in it, comfort. I now realize that I was compensating for the rest of my life, which was filled to the brim with microtechnology—computers, modems, faxes, the Internet—machines that I could operate but did not really understand. I was feeling detached, and I wanted to ground myself in a technology that I could control and intuit. The pinhole camera was just right; it supplied me with the feeling of operating a machine that I had built from scratch (from a shoebox), that I could adjust and fix, that needed no warranty.

The other thing about pinhole photography that really appealed to me was the severe limitation of information. I had no choice but to focus completely on one image at a time—no motor drive on this camera. I would expose one piece of paper and then develop it to see how it came out. It was a wonderfully liberating feeling not even to have the opportunity to be distracted. Though the amount of information created in an afternoon was minuscule (just a few small prints), it somehow mattered more than whole stacks of 35mm pictures. We have many boxes of these, but we rarely get them out. They are in packs of thirty-six exposures, with much duplication. Here I am walking along the outside of the cathedral. Here I am getting closer to the entrance of the cathedral. Here I am just inside. And so on. This more complete historical record is nice to have, but no single shot has the resonance that the pinhole pics have, in their isolation. The math is flipped upside down: One is more than thirty-six. In this case, less is truly more.

This enthusiasm for minimalism has spread in our household. My wife and I have made a habit out of using a Polaroid camera to document our lives, savoring the severe limitation. We take one picture at a time. We patiently wait for it to develop. We examine the picture and compare it to our life experience.

It costs more, but in our glutted environment that can be a very good thing, encouraging us to limit our use of the camera to one print per "event." Its expense means that I will take just one picture and I will cherish it. In a universe of speedy possibilities, it is a speedbump, a boundary for which I am grateful. We have in our kitchen a stack of Polaroids taken over the last several years, of house and dinner guests. One per. It is a compact and satisfying historical record. Each one captures one brief moment of an entire evening, and somehow seems just the right size record to help us conjure up the rest of the evening in our minds. It is a memory trigger, an aid, a point of reference.

George Mason University professor Hugh Heclo calls this return to more fundamental, resonant technologies "downteching," the conscious embrace of older, simpler machines. "Expect the downtech movement to grow," he says. "In the long run, excesses of technology mean that the comparative advantage shifts from those with information glut to those with ordered knowledge, from those who can process vast amounts of throughput to those who can explain what is worth knowing and why."

In line with Heclo's observation, there is a growing movement in this country called "voluntary simplicity" (inspired by a book of that name by Duane Elgin), which is dedicated to the pursuit of a more sustainable, balanced life. "To live more simply is to live more purposefully and with a minimum of needless distraction," writes Elgin. Sympathetic magazines and radio shows have been cropping up, endorsing the notion that, without forsaking technology, we should make an effort to use the most basic technologies available that can get the job done—preferably tools whose function anyone can plainly understand.

It is often said that we are on the cusp of a whole new age when intelligent machines will take over much of the work we do. I suspect that just the opposite may be true—that we are about to comprehend the true limitations of machines. Once we realize that information technology truly cannot replace human experience, that as it increases the available information it also helps devalue the meaning of each piece of information, we will be on the road to reasserting our dominance over technology.

chapter 21

De-nichify

How to change our electronic Tower of Babel into a modern Agora? The answer is easy, though the solution is not: We need to talk to one another. Recall Bill Bradley's challenge: "When was the last time you talked about race with someone of a different race? If the answer is never, you're part of the problem."

Radio talk show host Brian Lehrer has found a way to fuse some of our social fragments back together. Lehrer, host of WNYC's *On the Line* in New York City, is bucking the national trend toward specialization and nichification. He is a generalist, covering as wide a range of social and political issues as he possibly can, reaching out to different cultures and niches. Lehrer justifiably advertises his show as "dialogue, not diatribe."

One highlight of this effort is Lehrer's annual multicultural out-reach on Martin Luther King Day, when he invites listeners to call in and read one-minute excerpts from works about an ethnic group different from their own. The purpose is to force people to consider different life perspectives. It works.

The rest of the days are devoted to the simple notion that communities work better if people come together to discuss their differences. In a single two-hour show, Lehrer might conduct informed, professional, on-air conversations on Bosnia, teachers' unions, and date rape. In a glutted and specialized world, this is an increasingly difficult task, but also an increasingly important one. Generalists are working for a less-fragmented world of isolated experts, toward a world of common understanding.

With his format of dialogue, not diatribe, Brian Lehrer and his generalist brethren are shining a bright light out of the information muck by embracing the format of universal dialogue. Theirs is exactly the kind of regular effort that establishes a foundation of understanding and tolerance. As the information society fosters niches, all of us, whether we are media professionals or not, should make some effort to avoid letting our lives become completely segmented. Specialization is empowering and rejuvenating, but also inherently limiting. We can't all have our own radio show, but we can tune into such shows and read general interest magazines and newspapers; we can make a point to reach across niche boundaries; we can avoid specialized, exclusive jargon whenever possible; we can introduce ourselves to our neighbors regardless of whether they share our skin color, and we can attend more formal inter-ethnic forums. And, of course, we must take every opportunity speak out against ethnic intolerance.

As we reach across cultural boundaries and pursue interdisciplinary studies, we are pursuing the best kind of education—not just learning how to become more efficient at a specialized task, but how to interact with the rest of humanity. These sorts of pursuits enable us to embrace the joys of education as the best possible antidote to data smog. Education, as we have discussed, is anti-glut. It is the harnessing of information, organizing it into knowledge and memory. Education also breeds a healthy skepticism, and will help consumers fend off manipulative marketing tactics. Education is the one thing we can't get overloaded with. The more of it, the better.

chapter 22

Don't Forsake Government; Help Improve It

Finally, for collective fixes more appropriately enacted on behalf of all society, we must call on that awkward but thoroughly necessary beast, government.

Yes, *government*. Federal initiatives are badly needed, mostly because technology policy is too important to be surrendered to chance or to the wealthiest corporations. The cyberlibertarian community has made anti-government rhetoric a fashionable part of the information revolution, mostly in response to a lot of very thoughtless federal legislation. After a particularly stupid law was signed by President Clinton in 1996—the Communications Decency Act, which aimed to excessively curb speech online—leading cyber thinker John Perry Barlow issued a "Declaration of the Independence of Cyberspace," which rashly proclaimed the Net to be its own world, not a functioning part of conventional society:

Governments of the Industrial World, you weary giants of flesh and steel, I come from Cyberspace, the new home of Mind. On behalf of the future, I ask you of the past to leave us alone. You are not welcome among us. You have no sovereignty where we gather. . . . I declare the global social space we are building to be naturally independent of the tyrannies you seek to impose on us. You have no moral right to rule us . . .

As a technorealist, I respectfully dissent. The Net is not literally a new world vested with its own sovereignty; it is a new and exciting facet of society, created and subsidized by a democratic government that, for all of its well-publicized bungling and wastefulness, actually works pretty well. Barlow is absolutely correct in describing cyberspace as a very different organism from our physical world. Ultimately, though, the former must fall under the jurisdiction of the latter. Physical space is where we are born, where we require food and shelter and protection, and where we must govern ourselves as human beings.

So, as many people wittingly and unwittingly lend their enthusiasm for technology to political movements that enfeeble government, it is critical that we stand up for what is right. To get the good that technology has to offer without choking on the bad will take strong collective effort. We should redouble our efforts to root out bad government—Gingrich and friends can certainly help in this regard—and realize that protecting basic freedoms and values often means that government needs to be stronger, not weaker.

Tempting though it often is, we must resist the urge to snidely dismiss the relevance and utility of government. In fact, we must embrace our democratic government and what it stands for—a body created by the citizens in order to serve the interests of their collective society. Government is cumbersome and often frustrating, but it is also essential in the effort to protect a democratic nation, to maintain civility and to help its citizens prosper. In finance, labor, commerce, law, energy, communications, housing, and the environment, we have relied on government to help establish rules and standards for progress, safety, and fairness. I say this not as a reflexive supporter of bureaucracy, but because our public sector has endured an unwarranted bashing in recent years. Good government has helped to make the United States an unparalleled success story in the history of humankind.

There is a special wrinkle, though, in promulgating regulations for the information society. That wrinkle is the First Amendment to the U.S. Constitution: "Congress shall make no law respecting an establishment of religion, or prohibiting the free exercise thereof; or abridging the freedom of speech, or of the press; or the right of the people peaceably to assemble, and to petition the Government for a redress of grievances."

This is perhaps the most important distinction between conventional pollution and data smog. No one has an inalienable right to pour dioxin into the ground; legislating against it, therefore, is fairly straightforward. But the right to say and publish virtually anything is a sacred one in a free society. We can't—and wouldn't want to—infringe on personal or political expression. So, instead, we should seek to control some of its unsavory consequences, and rein in some of those who would use technology to abuse or exploit us. Here's some of what government can specifically do in this regard:

David Shenk's pie-in-the-sky legislative agenda:

The government should help citizens defend themselves against data spam. Our quality of life is seriously hampered by unsolicited phone calls, faxes, mail, and e-mail. We have a right not to be harassed, and there is a very simple solution. The Telephone Consumer Protection Act of 1991 made it illegal to use an auto-dialing phone machine or to make calls with a prerecorded voice. This law should now be amended to address the problem of junk e-mail by barring, among other things, software that automatically plucks e-mail addresses from all over cyberspace and indiscriminately includes them in marketing solicitations.

Furthermore, this new legislation should establish on behalf of all consumers a national, mandatory "do-not-disturb" registry of names, phone numbers, addresses, and e-mail addresses by which all mass-marketers would be legally obliged to abide. Current do-not-disturb lists (featured in Appendix B) are voluntary. How would you like to never get a sales call at home again (eat your meals in peace for the rest of your days)? You could simply register your name and phone number on this one list. If you wish to keep your e-mail box free of garbage, add it to the same list. Marketers would be *required* to cross-reference their lists with the national do-not-disturb list and delete all matches before launching their sale barrages.

Cities and states should guarantee refuge from data smog. Excessive stimulus takes its social toll, and we must begin to compensate for this loss by severely restricting advertising and other noisy intrusions into our common spaces. Libraries and parks will not suffice as the only havens from the noise and commercial glut. As people begin to recognize the importance of glut-free rooms and roads, local governments will respond by designating "Zones of Quiet."

Vermont has already taken the lead in this regard by prohibiting advertising billboards on all highways, an action that makes traveling in that state a great luxury.* Which will be the first state to take the brave and important step of banning all advertising in schools?

The federal government can also play a role. In 1964, in response to the rapid industrialization and settlement expansion in the U.S., Congress passed the Wilderness Act, designating certain areas legally secure from the ravages of civilization. Wilderness areas were henceforth "secure for the American people of present and future generations." In the emerging information society, we now require

---

* Unfortunately, Vermont's tight restrictions on commercialism are not likely to be the wave of the future. The momentum seems to be on the other end of the spectrum, with cities like Atlanta taking the lead in leasing advertising space on city streets and other city property. "We're sitting, as most cities are, with thousands of non-income-producing assets that can easily be converted into income-producing assets," explains Atlanta adman Joel Babbitt.

analogous protections from information. A federal "Zones of Quiet Act" should forever stanch the flow of advertising into public spaces.

Prohibit government agencies and companies from using information for unauthorized purposes. To combat dataveillance, we need a sweeping new privacy law, an upgrade of The Federal Privacy Act of 1974. The new legislation should live up to the core principle of the previous law (subsequently gutted by other laws): *Information collected for one purpose should not be used for another purpose, unless and until specific permission is granted by the individual involved.* This time, the law should exempt no one.

In 1988, after a list of Judge Robert Bork's video rentals made it into the press, Congress hastily passed the Video Privacy Protection Act, barring video rental stores from releasing information about their customers' choices. This means that as you read this, your video records have a higher degree of legal protection than your medical records. The new law should remove the inequity by extending real privacy to *all* transactions. Whether you are subscribing to a magazine, buying a modem, renewing your driver's license, taking a random drug test, enrolling your child in school, or paying your taxes, you should be assured that the personal data you turn over will go no further than that particular institution. All information should be presumed confidential unless permission to the contrary is granted.

The FTC should root out consumer fraud and improve efforts at consumer education. It is time for the government to become a full-fledged consumer advocate. The vast majority of Americans are concerned with deception in ads, and favor more regulation. But the government has never been very responsive to this concern. Because political campaigns in this country are financed largely by corporations, politicians frequently forget that they are supposed to be working on behalf of consumers.

Now, because of increased distraction, the consumer is more vulnerable than ever to manipulative advertising. A new Consumer Education Act should remedy this by beefing up the Federal Trade Commission, the agency in charge of overseeing advertising claims.

The FTC's current policy is that consumers must match their wits against advertisers. When it comes to "half truths and motivational manipulations," writes *Advertising Age* columnist Stanley E. Cohen, "the remedy is *caveat emptor.*" Considering the resources and sophistication of marketers, this hardly seems a fair fight. We need an FTC that behaves more like the Food and Drug Administration did under the leadership of former Commissioner David Kessler. During his tenure, Kessler turned the FDA into an aggressive, proactive agency that fights for the health and safety of consumers. A similarly proactive FTC would criticize questionable marketing practices and would impose fines and embarrassing press coverage on the offenders.

A rejuvenated FTC should also thoroughly explore the health consequences (physical and psychological) of television, computers, and other advanced technologies, and should begin an aggressive consumer education campaign that follows the trail blazed by groups like Consumer's Union and Center for Science in the Public Interest. To be sure, comprehensive consumer protection is a complicated chore, with often imperfect results. But managed well, government agencies can do far more good than harm in this area.

All government documents should not only be accessible, but approachable. In our glutted society, government has a special responsibility to communicate with its citizens concisely and articulately. Tax forms are not the only documents that should be able to fit on a postcard. The essence of legislation, regulations, and court rulings should also be something that any literate person can understand. A new Government Information Act should insure that citizens have not just online access, but actual understanding of the workings of the government.

Reformulate the issue of "information have-nots." Much political hay has been made of late about the danger of the widening gap between the "information haves and have-nots." "If we allow the information superhighway to bypass the less fortunate sectors of our society, even for an interim period," Al Gore has warned, "we will find that the information rich will get richer while the information poor get poorer with no guarantee that everyone will be on the network at some future date."

Gore and other politicians are sadly missing the point. The disenfranchised citizens of our country are not in need of faster access to bottomless wells of information. They are in need of *education*. There is an important difference, and government must recognize this distinction soon. Jonathan Kozol has written eloquently of the inequities that underlie the crisis in our educational system. The so-called information poor don't need Internet access; they need basic classroom materials, building infrastructure, and highly qualified teachers.

In fact, the information superhighway is not only not a priority for the educational underclass—but, in a variety of ways already detailed in this book, access to such an abundance will create new problems for it. Indeed, as the educated elite learns to respond intelligently to the new challenges of data smog, it is the have-nots who will be additionally disadvantaged. "Just like the elite have taught themselves to diet in the face of food abundance," says sociologist András Szántó, "in the future, elites are more likely to express their tastes through purging the data around them. To be involved in a data purge culture will be to show that you are a sophisticated user of data, that you know where it comes from, you know how to pick up on the little info that matters and to how to get rid of the rest. This has already started to happen. It has become an elite act not to watch network TV or not to videotape your wedding."

Meanwhile, he says, "The sad irony of the information age is that the have-nots are going to end up with the data dumped on them."

The best way to prevent such a data smog gap from settling in is to shift the attention and resources toward basic educational infrastructure for all Americans.

Consensus conferences on technology policy. Finally, and most important, we need to overhaul the way we develop all technology policy. This would be a formidable challenge if it were not for the fact that a wonderful working model already exists right across the ocean.

In 1987 the Danish parliament came upon a fix for the perennially antidemocratic nature of technology policy. Traditionally, because of technology's inherent complexity, only technologists from the military, businesses, and universities have been invited into the policy-making process. For democracies like Denmark and the United States, this has frequently led to needless confusion and unrest. Nuclear power, bovine growth hormone, and food irradiation are just three of many instances where closed-door policy formulations have backfired after they were put into place. Not letting ordinary people confront the implications of policies until they are implemented is like deciding to bake an apple pie in order to find out if your friend is allergic to apples.

There is a better way, and Denmark has found it: consensus conferences. Consensus conferences establish a natural bridge between technologists, policy-makers, and ordinary citizens. The Danish Board of Technology recruits a diverse group of citizens, who are promptly immersed in one particular issue facing the parliament (genetic testing, for example). As a rule, the citizen panel contains no technical experts and no representatives from relevant interest groups. Panelists are supplied with necessary background material and asked to make specific policy recommendations on a pending matter of biotechnology or information technology. After two weekends of deliberation, the panel is convened for a four-day public forum in which the citizens hear testimony of experts and interest groups, cross-examine the experts, deliberate, and finally issue a report and conduct a press conference.

"It is a lovely process that has stimulated broad popular discussions and influenced Parliamentary decisions," says the Loka Institute's Richard Sclove, who has closely studied the Danish approach. The reports, he says, are "clearly reasoned, and nuanced in judgment. . . . [portions] can be incisive and impassioned as well, especially in comparison with the circumspection and dry language that is conventional in expert policy analyses."

Now the Loka Institute, an Amherst, Massachusetts–based think tank specializing in technology policy, is spearheading a worthwhile effort to persuade the U.S. to adopt such a system. With respect both to policy and public awareness, the idea makes a lot of sense. The consensus conference represents precisely the kind of paradigm this nation must embrace in our new age of electronic democracy, in order to make citizen knowledge commensurate with the power of their opinions (as registered in polls). Above all else, it is imperative that in the coming years we strive to keep the quality of our thinking as great as the quantity of our information.

Acknowledgments

This book is a quilt of intelligence. I will take full responsibility for its shortcomings, but the credit for its wisdom must be spread across the hundreds of people I have had the fortune to speak to, correspond with, and read. I'd like now to thank some of those behind the text.

I am deeply indebted to draft readers Ellen Abbott, Jeremy Benjamin, Eric Berlow, Joanne Cohen, Sidney Cohen, Bonni Cohen, Shari Cohen, Brian Hecht, Hank Klibanoff, Roy Kreitner, Jon Shenk, Rob Snyder, Mitch Stephens, and András Szántó for their astute criticism and constructive advice.

Virtually every page in this book was improved by the tireless editing and fiery intelligence of my brother Joshua Wolf Shenk.

Richard Shenk has been this book's bedrock supporter for longer than either of us would like to be reminded. His determination is my determination.

I received critical assistance from my friends Dean Blackketter, Sue Cook, Bruce Feiler, Kurt Hirsch, John Holzman, Gawain Kripke,

Gersh Kuntzman, Hugh Lefcort, Steve Silberman, and Sarah Williams.

Research for this book was underwritten by a fellowship at the Freedom Forum Media Studies Center, at Columbia University. I am grateful to Everette Dennis, Larry McGill, Nancy Hicks Maynard, Nancy Woodhull, Adam Clayton Powell III, and the rest of the terrific staff and my inspiring fellow fellows. John Arbo made this a much more thorough and factual work, with help from Carl Haacke. I also thank the libraries of the Freedom Forum, American University, Columbia University, Rubenstein–Markiewicz, and 1805 Quincy Street. This project received generous assistance from America Online; and I want to thank LEXIS–NEXIS, a division of Reed Elsevier, Inc., for the use of the LEXIS–NEXIS services in the preparation of this book.

Sloan Harris at ICM and Eamon Dolan at HarperCollins are the two publishing soul mates I have been searching for. They are as kind and generous as they are smart. I am eternally grateful for their confidence, their counsel, and most of all for making this serious endeavor such a pleasurable one.

A great spiritual debt is owed to Keith Jarrett for his solo piano recordings. Jerry Garcia lifted up these pages before and after his death.

Finally, to my wife and best friend, Alexandra Beers, who put her brains and heart into this book and who helped me evolve along with it: my eternal gratitude and all my love.

Appendix A: Technorealism—An Overview

In this heady age of rapid technological change, we all struggle to maintain our bearings. The developments that unfold each day in communications and computing can be thrilling and disorienting. One understandable reaction is to wonder: Are these changes good or bad? Should we welcome or fear them?

The answer is both. Technology is making life more convenient and enjoyable, and many of us healthier, wealthier, and wiser. But it is also affecting work, family, and the economy in unpredictable ways, introducing new forms of tension and distraction, and posing new threats to the cohesion of our physical communities.

Despite the complicated and often contradictory implications of technology, the conventional wisdom is woefully simplistic. Pundits, politicians, and self-appointed visionaries do us a disservice when they try to reduce these complexities to breathless tales of either high-tech doom or cyber-elation. Such polarized thinking leads to dashed hopes and unnecessary anxiety, and prevents us from understanding our own culture.

ie past few years, even as the debate over technology has ninated by the louder voices at the extremes, a new, more d consensus has quietly taken shape. This document seeks to ate some of the shared beliefs behind that consensus, which ive come to call technorealism.

Technorealism demands that we think critically about the role that tools and interfaces play in human evolution and everyday life. Integral to this perspective is our understanding that the current tide of technological transformation, while important and powerful, is actually a continuation of waves of change that have taken place throughout history. Looking, for example, at the history of the automobile, television, or the telephone—not just the devices but the institutions they became—we see profound benefits as well as substantial costs. Similarly, we anticipate mixed blessings from today's emerging technologies, and expect to forever be on guard for unexpected consequences—which must be addressed by thoughtful design and appropriate use.

As technorealists, we seek to expand the fertile middle ground between techno-utopianism and neo-Luddism. We are technology "critics" in the same way, and for the same reasons, that others are food critics, art critics, or literary critics. We can be passionately optimistic about some technologies, skeptical and disdainful of others. Still, our goal is neither to champion nor dismiss technology, but rather to understand it and apply it in a manner more consistent with basic human values.

Below are some evolving basic principles that help explain technorealism.

Principles of Technorealism

1. Technologies are not neutral.
A great misconception of our time is the idea that technologies are completely free of bias—that because they are inanimate artifacts, they don't promote certain kinds of behaviors over others. In truth,

technologies come loaded with both intended and unintended social, political, and economic leanings. Every tool provides its users
with a particular manner of seeing the world and specific ways of
interacting with others. It is important for each of us to consider the
biases of various technologies and to seek out those that reflect our
values and aspirations.

2. The Internet is revolutionary, but not Utopian.

The Net is an extraordinary communications tool that provides a
range of new opportunities for people, communities, businesses,
and government. Yet as cyberspace becomes more populated, it increasingly resembles society at large, in all its complexity. For every
empowering or enlightening aspect of the wired life, there will also
be dimensions that are malicious, perverse, or rather ordinary.

3. Government has an important role to play on the electronic frontier.

Contrary to some claims, cyberspace is not formally a place or jurisdiction separate from Earth. While governments should respect
the rules and customs that have arisen in cyberspace, and should
not stifle this new world with inefficient regulation or censorship, it
is foolish to say that the public has no sovereignty over what an er-
rant citizen or fraudulent corporation does online. As the representative of the people and the guardian of democratic values, the state
has the right and responsibility to help integrate cyberspace and
conventional society.

Technology standards and privacy issues, for example, are too
important to be entrusted to the marketplace alone. Competing
software firms have little interest in preserving the open standards
that are essential to a fully functioning interactive network. Markets
encourage innovation, but they do not necessarily insure the public
interest.

4. Information is not knowledge.

All around us, information is moving faster and becoming cheaper
to acquire, and the benefits are manifest. That said, the proliferation
of data is also a serious challenge, requiring new measures of

human discipline and skepticism. We must not confuse the thrill of acquiring or distributing information quickly with the more daunting task of converting it into knowledge and wisdom. Regardless of how advanced our computers become, we should never use them as a substitute for our own basic cognitive skills of awareness, perception, reasoning, and judgment.

5. Wiring the schools will not save them.

The problems with America's public schools—disparate funding, social promotion, bloated class size, crumbling infrastructure, lack of standards—have almost nothing to do with technology. Consequently, no amount of technology will lead to the educational revolution prophesied by President Clinton and others. The art of teaching cannot be replicated by computers, the Net, or by "distance learning." These tools can, of course, augment an already high quality educational experience. But to rely on them as any sort of panacea would be a costly mistake.

6. Information wants to be protected.

It's true that cyberspace and other recent developments are challenging our copyright laws and frameworks for protecting intellectual property. The answer, though, is not to scrap existing statutes and principles. Instead, we must update old laws and interpretations so that information receives roughly the same protection it did in the context of old media. The goal is the same: to give authors sufficient control over their work so that they have an incentive to create, while maintaining the right of the public to make fair use of that information. In neither context does information want "to be free." Rather, it needs to be protected.

7. The public owns the airwaves; the public should benefit from their use.

The recent digital spectrum giveaway to broadcasters underscores the corrupt and inefficient misuse of public resources in the arena of technology. The citizenry should benefit and profit from the use of public frequencies, and should retain a portion of the spectrum for educational, cultural, and public access uses. We should demand more for private use of public property.

8. Understanding technology is an essential component of global citizenship.

In a world driven by the flow of information, the interfaces—and the underlying code—that make information visible are becoming enormously powerful social forces. Understanding their strengths and limitations, and even participating in the creation of better tools, should be an important part of being an involved citizen. These tools affect our lives as much as laws do, and we should subject them to a similar democratic scrutiny.

Signed (in alphabetical order),

DAVID S. BENNAHUM, New York, New York
Contributing editor, *Wired*
Contributing editor, *Spin*

BROOKE SHELBY BIGGS, San Francisco, California
Columnist, *San Francisco Bay Guardian* online

PAULINA BORSOOK, San Francisco, California
Author, *Cyberselfish: Technolibertarianism and the True Revenge of the Nerds* (forthcoming from Broadway books)

MARISA BOWE, New York, New York
Editor-in-Chief, *Word*
Former Conference Manager, ECHO

SIMSON GARFINKEL, Vineyard Haven, Massachusetts
Contributing writer, *Wired*
Columnist, *The Boston Globe*

STEVEN JOHNSON, New York, New York
Author, *Interface Culture: How New Technology Transforms the Way We Create and Communicate*
Editor-in-chief, *Feed*

DOUGLAS RUSHKOFF, New York, New York
Author, *Cyberia, Media Virus, Playing the Future,* and *Ecstasy Club*
Columnist, *New York Times Syndicate,* Time Digital

ANDREW L. SHAPIRO, Cambridge, Massachusetts
Fellow, Harvard Law School's Berkman Center for Internet & Society
Contributing editor, *The Nation*

DAVID SHENK, Brooklyn, New York
Author, *Data Smog: Surviving the Information Glut*
Commentator, National Public Radio

STEVE SILBERMAN, San Francisco, California
Senior Culture Writer, *Wired News*

MARK STAHLMAN, New York, New York
Author, *The Battle for Cyberspace* (forthcoming)
Co-founder, New York New Media Association

STEFANIE SYMAN, New York, New York
Executive editor and co-founder, *Feed*

Appendix B: How to Get Off Junk Mail/Phone Lists

1. To reduce the amount of national advertising mail you receive at home, send a request to be removed from all mailing lists along with your name, variations on your name (for example, Roy Biv, Roy G. Biv, R. Biv, and so on) and your address to:

    Mail Preference Service
    Direct Marketing Association
    P.O. Box 9008
    Farmingdale, NY 11735–9008

    and to:

    Experian Opt Out
    701 Experian Parkway
    Allen, TX 75002

    (Experian also offers a dial-up alternative: 1–800–353–0809)

    Experian will take you off their list and off those of two other credit bureaus, Equifax Options and Trans Union.

2. To reduce the amount of national advertising calls you receive at home, send your name, address, area code, and telephone number to:

   Telephone Preference Service
   Direct Marketing Association
   P.O. Box 9014
   Farmingdale, NY 11735–9014

   (Names remain on Direct Marketing Association lists for five years. After five years, you will need to register with these lists again.)

3. To have your name and e-mail address removed from all electronic commercial mailing lists controlled by Cyber Promotions, send an e-mail to: remove@cyberpromo.com, with the words "REMOVE ALL" in the subject or message field.

4. To remove your e-mail address from other junk e-mail lists, follow the instructions provided in each particular solicitation.

Sources and Notes

Page 7: *Mr. Mouche quote:* Moebius and Jean-Luc Coudray, *Monsieur Mouche,* He'lyode (Brussels, Belgium: He'lyode Press, 1994).

Preface

Page 15: *Kennedy quote:* address given at National Academy of Sciences, Washington D.C., October 22, 1963.

Part I

Page 17: *Postman quote: Utne Reader,* July–August 1995; 35. (Originally from a speech given earlier that year at Town Hall, in New York City.)

Page 17: *"In the information age, there can be too much exposure . . . ":* The *New York Times,* September 23, 1995.

Chapter 1

Page 21: *Brian Lamb:* lecture at Columbia University, October 17, 1995.

Page 24: *Richard Meier:* Richard Meier, *A Communications Theory of Urban Growth* (Cambridge, MA: MIT Press, 1962); 132. Referenced in Orrin Klapp, *Overload and Boredom* (New York: Greenwood Press, 1986); 7.

Page 24: *Spam:* K. K. Campbell, "Chatting with Martha Siegel," http://www.eff.org/pub/Legal/Cases/Canter_Siegel/c-and-s_summary.article. (Spam is an acronym, standing for spiced pork and ham.)

Page 26: *"Tens of thousands of words . . . ":* Philip Novak, from a commencement address at Dominican College, San Rafael, California, 1988. Published in *Dominican Quarterly,* Summer 1988.

Page 26: *"In the shop window . . . ":* Italo Calvino, *If on a winter's night a traveler,* English translation (New York: Harcourt Brace Jovanovitch, 1981); 4, 5.

Page 26: *"One weekday edition of today's* New York Times *. . . ":* Theodore Roszak, *The Cult of Information: The Folklore of Computers and the True*

Art of Thinking (New York: Pantheon, 1986); 32. (Referenced in Eli M. Noam, "Visions of the Media Age: Taming the Information Monster," in *Multimedia: A Revolutionary Challenge.* Third Annual Colloquium, June 16/17, 1995 [Frankfurt am Main: Schaffer-Poeschel Verlag Stuttgart, 1995]; 21.)

Page 27: *"the actual act of finding something . . . ":* Frank Beacham, "Information Without Experience," from the syndicated column "Questioning Technology," http://www.beacham.com/info_glut_914.html.

Page 28: *abruptly knocked off track:* Noam, "Visions of the Media Age"; 18–19.

Page 28: *"information discrepancy":* Jaako Lehtonen, "The Information Society and the New Competence," *American Behavioral Scientist,* November/December 1988; 104–11.

Page 28: *Adoption of information technologies:* technology penetration data courtesy of The Weidt Group. (Data originally obtained from *The Minneapolis/St. Paul Star Tribune.*)

Page 28: *In 1850:* Klapp, *Overload and Boredom;* 7.

Page 29: *Most Americans handle information:* Louise Sweeney, *The Christian Science Monitor,* January 26, 1978; 26. (Klapp, *Overload and Boredom;* 7.)

Page 29: *computer processing speed has doubled:* Robert E. Calem, *The New York Times* on the Web, February 14, 1996. "We'll be at one million times faster [than ENIAC] in six years if Moore's Law continues to hold true, which it always has," said Prof. Mitchell Marcus, chairman of Moore's Computer and Information Science Department.

Page 29: *Information has become more dense: TV Dimensions '95 & Magazine Dimensions '95.*

Page 29: *"The real issue . . . ":* Noam, "Visions of the Media Age"; 18–19.

Page 30: *Michael Dertouzos: Technology Review,* August/September 1994.

Page 30: *560 daily advertising messages . . . :* Noam, "Visions of the Media Age"; 28.

Page 30: *60 percent:* Patrick Ames, *Beyond Paper* (Indianapolis: Hayden Press, 1993).

Page 30: *paper consumption:* Jeff Davidson. "The Frantic Society," *Business and Society Review* 83, September 22, 1992; 4. (Noam, "Visions of the Media Age"; 22.)

Page 31: *third-class mail:* Noam, "Visions of the Media Age"; 20–24.

Page 31: *Two-thirds of business managers . . . :* "Dying for Information? An investigation into the effects of information overload in the UK and worldwide." Study conducted by Dr. David Lewis, published by *Reuters Business Information,* October 1996.

Page 31: *More than 1,000 telemarketing companies . . . :* Cristina Rouvalis, "Charm, Persistence and a Telephone," *Pittsburgh Post-Gazette,* May 25, 1997.

Page 32: *"Is it crass? . . . ":* Peter Applebome, "How Atlanta's Adman Pushes the City to Sell Itself," *The New York Times,* February 9, 1993; A16.

Chapter 2

Page 35: *Prometheus:* Robert Graves, *The Greek Myths: 1* (New York: Penguin, 1960); 144–45.

Page 35: *techne:* Philip Novak, "Plato and the Computer," in P. J. Umphrey, ed., *The Thread of Ariadne* (Fort Bragg, CA: Q.E.D. Press, 1988); 37–50.

Page 35: *Three out of four Americans complain of chronic stress:* "The Mitchum Report on Stress in the 90s." (76 percent). Also: "The Annals of Internal Medicine recently reported that 24 percent of people surveyed complained of fatigue that lasts longer than two weeks. Fatigue is now among the top five reasons people call the doctor. People are frayed by the inescapable pressure of technology, frazzled by the lack of time for themselves, their families, their PTAs and church groups," *Newsweek,* March 6, 1995.

Page 36: *Two out of every three visits . . . :* Claudia Wallis, "Stress: Can We Cope?" *Time,* June 6, 1983; 48.

Page 36: *three top-selling prescription drugs . . . :* "The Leading 100 Prescription Drugs by U.S. Sales," *Med Ad News,* May 1995; 22. (The drugs are Zantac, Prozac, and Procardia.)

Page 36: *Stress is also partly to blame . . . :* Daniel Goleman, "A Rising Cost of Modernity: Depression," *The New York Times,* December 8, 1992.

Page 36: *"People seem to be developing a form of ADD without inheriting it . . . ":* Evan I. Schwartz, "Interrupt-Driven," *Wired,* June 1994; 46.

Page 36: *"official brain syndrome of the information age":* Schwartz, "Interrupt-Driven." (Emphasis on *society* is mine.)

Page 37: *Increased cardiovascular stress:* J. H. Ettema and R. L. Zielhuis,

"Physiological Parameters of Mental Load," *Ergonomics* 14, 1971; 137–44. (Also: P. R. Boyce, "Sinus Arrhythmia as a Measure of Mental Load," *Ergonomics* 17, 1974; 177–83.)

Page 37: *Weakened vision:* "Unless we do something about it," says Japanese medical professor Tetsu Ishikawa, "the day is coming when all 100 million [Japanese] will be nearsighted." Japan has even had to lower some aviation eyesight standards to accommodate the decline. *The Mainichi Daily News,* March 15, 1995.

Page 37: *Confusion:* Naresh K. Malhotra, "Reflections on the Information Overload Paradigm in Consumer Decision Making," *Journal of Consumer Research* 10, March 1984; 438.

Page 38: *Frustration:* James Rotten, Donald Olszewski, Marc Charleton, and Edgardo Soler, "Loud Speech, Conglomerate Noise, and Behavioral Aftereffects," *Journal of Applied Psychology* 63, no. 3, 1978; 360–65.

Page 38: *Impaired judgment:* Siegfried Streufert, et al., "Components of Response Rate in Complex Decision Making," *Journal of Experimental Social Psychology* 3, 1967; 286–95, especially 292. (Also, Jacob Jacoby, "Information Load and Decision Quality: Some Contested Issues," *Journal of Marketing Research* 14, November 1977; 569–73.)

Page 38: *Decreased benevolence:* Charles Korte, Ido Ypma, and Anneke Toppen, "Helpfulness in Dutch Society as a Function of Urbanization and Environmental Input Level," *Journal of Personality and Social Psychology* 32, 1975; 996–1003. (Also, D. Sherrod and R. Downs, "Environmental Determinants of Altruism: The Effects of Stimulus Overload and Perceived Control on Helping," *Journal of Experimental Social Psychology* 10, 1974; 468–79.)

Page 38: *Overconfidence:* T. R. Stewart, W. R. Moninger, K. F. Heideman, and P. Reagan-Cirincione, "Effects of Improved Information on the Components of Skill in Weather Forecasting," *Organizational Behavior and Human Decision Processes* 53, 1992; 107–34. (This is supported by Duke University's John Payne: "While the quality in judgment doesn't go up that much, the confidence in judgment goes up quite a bit. So you think you're doing better, although you really aren't. . . . So you really get a disconnect between how confident people feel in the decision they made, and actually how accurate they are. They become overconfident." Author interview.)

Page 38: *Stanley Milgram:* Stanley Milgram, "The Experience of Living in the Cities," *Science,* March 13, 1970; 1461–68.

Page 39: *"Helpfulness shown toward a stranger . . . ":* Korte, Ypma, and Toppen, "Helpfulness in Dutch Society."

Page 40: *"My idea of pure bliss . . . ":* Bruce Tracy, senior editor at Doubleday. Phone interview, February 14, 1995.

Page 40: *Communications have been the lifeblood . . . :* Stephen Saxby, *The Age of Information* (New York: New York University Press, 1990); 19–21.

Page 41: *"For [mankind], the main troubles will stem . . . ":* Desmond Morris, *The Naked Ape* (New York: McGraw-Hill, 1967); 48.

Page 41: *Peppered Moth;* scientific name: *Biston betularia.* Information supplied by Hugh Lefcort, assistant professor of biology, Gonzaga University.

Page 42: *volume and speed of information . . . :* Ed Leary, "Amino Acids: The Future of Computing in the 1990s," *Journal of Systems Management* 40, no. 12, December 1989; 23.

Page 42: *"Because technology can evolve . . . ":* Robert Cialdini, *Influence: The Psychology of Persuasion* (New York: William Morrow, 1993); 277.

Page 42: *"There I was . . . ":* phone interview, 1995.

Page 43: *"Personally, the speed . . .":* Jon Wallis, senior lecturer in information systems, Engineering School of Computing & IT, University of Wolverhampton, UK. Via e-mail.

Page 43: *"computer work is like a drug . . . ":* Rolf Diederichs.

Page 44: *giving up a finger:* phone interview with Phillip Nicholson, founder of the Technostress Information Network.

Page 45: *"I felt strangely hyperactive . . . ":* phone interview.

Page 46: *"antennae of the race . . . ":* Ezra Pound reference in Marshall McLuhan, *The Medium Is the Message,* 2d ed. (New York: Signet, 1964); Introduction, xi.

Page 46: *166 pages of articles:* The downloads took up roughly one megabyte of memory on my hard drive. A byte being roughly equivalent to one character, six thousand per page, means that one megabyte is about 166 pages of text.

Page 48: *"They are not in a stage . . . ":* Maryln Schwartz, "Forgetful? Relax; You're Not Alone," *The Dallas Morning News,* March 18, 1993; 1C.

Page 48: *"We're exceptional at storing information . . . ":* phone interview, April 1995.

Chapter 3

Page 52: *Hi-tech revenue for Washington State:* gross business income for SIC code 737, Washington State Department of Revenue. Data provided by Jeff Olsen.

Page 52: *"low-friction, low-overhead capitalism . . . ":* from the press material of Bill Gates, *The Road Ahead* (New York: Viking, 1995).

Page 52: *$1 trillion in annual revenue:* Catherine Arnst, "Deregulation Is Launching a $1 Trillion Digital Free-for-All," *Business Week,* April 8, 1996; 64.

Page 53: *The great propagandists of our time have understood . . . :* Russell Jacoby, "Can We Talk?" *The Washington Post,* June 26, 1994. "They overwhelmed the individual with loud music, speeches and pictures. . . . Modern advertisers know this also. No one can compete with million-dollar television commercials; the mix of sound and image is simply too slick and seductive."

Page 54: *Malaleuca:* Tom Kelly, "I Think That I Shall Never See a Plant as Malignant as Florida's Punk Tree," *The Fort Lauderdale Sun-Sentinel,* March 17, 1995; 19A.

Page 55: *"dense TV":* New York University Professor Mitchell Stephens vehemently disagrees with this proposition, arguing in his upcoming book *The Rise of the Image/The Fall of the Word* (Oxford University Press) that we are quite possibly venturing into a new age of dense *and* progressive television.

Page 55: *One-half of all large North American companies . . . : Information Week,* April 1, 1996; 22.

Page 55: *"It's like an atomic bomb":* Peter H. Lewis, "Computers Beware! New Type of Virus Is Loose on the Net," *The New York Times,* September 4, 1995. (*Wired* magazine reminds us in its "Scared Shitlist" that it isn't just *like* an atomic bomb. It also *is* an atomic bomb: Suitcase-sized nuclear weapons are one of many nightmare technologies, along with plutonium tap water and electromagnetic pulse bombs that disable electrical current, that are now emerging as realistic possibilities, January 1995; 110.)

Page 55: *Barlow:* from seminar given at the Freedom Forum Media Studies Center.

Page 56: *Juliet Schor: Vital Speeches,* October 1, 1994.

Page 56: *"technology may be your enemy":* John Ydstie, "The Growing Inequality of Incomes in America, Part 1," National Public Radio, *Morning Edition,* February 27, 1996.

Page 56: *toxic gas leaks:* A toxic Union Carbide gas leak was caused by an improperly programmed computer. From the front page of *The New York Times,* August 14 and 24, 1985, as reported in the RISKS forum.

Page 57: *RISKS:* http://catless.ncl.ac.uk/Risks.data/info.html.

Page 57: *"There are going to be some governments . . . ":* Ellen Perlman, "The Year Zero: When the Computers Fail to Roll Over," Scripps Howard News Service, September 28, 1996.

Chapter 4

Page 59: *"There has to be a missionary spirit . . . ":* Jeffrey Klein, "Editor's Note," *Mother Jones,* March/April 1995; 3.

Page 60: *"destined to provide greater knowledge . . . ":* David Sarnoff, Foreword to Lenox R. Lohr, *Television Broadcasting* (New York: McGraw-Hill, 1940).

Page 60: *The average child watches 22,000 hours . . . :* Don Oldenburg, "Boob Tube Brain Drain? Probing TV's Influence on Young Minds," *The Washington Post,* October 12, 1992; D5.

Page 60: *"I expect education of all kinds . . . ":* Bill Gates, *The Road Ahead;* Chapter 9. http://www.roadahead.com/cChap9.htm

Page 62: *More on techno-utopianism:* "The government, and others, construct utopian tales about these technologies to render them socially meaningful and to mobilize large-scale support," write researchers Iacono and Kling. "People's hopes are renewed by the promise of new technology. In fact, however, we know little about how computer networking will be deployed, who will benefit and who will lose." Suzanne Iacono and Rob Kling, "Computerization Movements and Tales of Technological Utopianism," from *Computerization and Controversy: Value Conflicts and Social Choices,* 2d ed., edited by Rob Kling (Academic Press, 1995).

Page 63: *another economic depression was widely expected:* J. Merton England, *A Patron for Pure Science: The National Science Foundation's Formative Years, 1945–1957* (Washington, D.C.: National Science Foundation, 1982); 108.

Page 63: *"Without scientific progress . . . ":* England, *A Patron for Pure Science;* 107–8.

Page 64: *A revolution was on its way:* Larry Owens, "The Counterproductive Management of Science in the Second World War: Vannevar Bush and the Office of Scientific Research and Development; Experts, War, and the State," *Business History Review,* December 22, 1994.

Page 64: *"super-organization of Matter upon itself . . . ":* Pierre Teilhard de Chardin, *The Future of Man* (New York: Harper & Row, 1964); 132. (Original French copyright, 1959.) John Perry Barlow calls Teilhard de Chardin's vision of a Noosphere "The Great Work."

Page 64: *"standing editorial organization . . . ":* H. G. Wells, *World Brain* (London: Adadmintine Press, 1994); 88. (From http://wire.co.uk/trend-monitor/wb0.htm.)

Page 65: *several new viruses are now created every day:* Peter H. Lewis, "Computers Beware! New Type of Virus Is Loose on the Net," *The New York Times,* September 4, 1995; 1.

Page 65: *in 1940 only 38.1 percent . . . :* U.S. Department of Commerce, Bureau of the Census (via World Wide Web). In 1900 only 7 percent of all fourteen- to seventeen-year-olds attended high school; by 1960, 90 percent did so.

Page 65: *"The ultimate irony of [our] findings . . . ":* Andrew Kohut, "The Age of Indifference: A Study of Young Americans and How They View the News," Times Mirror Center for The People & The Press, June 28, 1990.

Page 66: *"In a survey of 2,100 college students . . . ":* survey by John Cronin, a molecular geneticist at the University of California at San Francisco, and Alan Almquist, a professor at California State University at Hayward.

Page 67: *was the Soviet Union ever an ally of the United States:* ABC News; 1,504 participants, February 6, 1986.

Page 67: *does Kuwait have a democratic or undemocratic system . . . :* The *Los Angeles Times,* March 9, 1991.

Page 67: *The Unchanging American Voter:* Eric Smith, *The Unchanging American Voter* (Berkeley: University of California Press, 1989); 4.

Page 67: *"Americans' innocence of political knowledge . . . ":* Stephen Bennett, "'Know-nothings' Revisited: The Meaning of Political Ignorance Today," *Social Science Quarterly,* June 1988; 476–90. (Italics mine.)

Page 69: *"The IBM is a machine . . . ":* Steven Levy, *Insanely Great* (New York: Viking, 1994); 163.

Page 70: *"The purpose of this design . . . ":* Levy, *Insanely Great;* 111.

Page 71: *"Do you want to sell sugar water . . . ":* film, *Triumph of the Nerds: The Rise of Accidental Empires,* aired on PBS, 1996.

Page 72: *"A revolution is under way . . . ":* Merrill Sheils, "And Man Created the Chip," *Newsweek,* June 30, 1980. (Emphasis mine.)

Page 72: *"Within a few years . . . "*: John Cassidy, "Tolls Could Be Costly on Info Superhighway," *The New York Post*, October 14, 1993.

Page 73: *"We can revolutionize education . . . "*: remarks by the President, Old Central New Jersey Railroad Terminal, Liberty State Park, Jersey City, New Jersey, May 7, 1996. (Accessed on the White House website: http://library.whitehouse.gov.)

Page 73: *"There are thousands of buildings in this country . . . "*: Hundt was quoted by Al Gore, in a speech at the National Press Club, December 21, 1993.

Page 74: *"Perhaps the saddest occasion for me . . . "*: Alan Kay, "Powerful Ideas Need Love Too!" written remarks to Joint Hearing on Educational Technology in the Twenty-First Century, Science Committee and the Economic Educational Opportunities Committee, U.S. House of Representatives, October 12, 1995. Washington, D.C. (Accessed from http://www.research.apple.com/people/features/congress_speech.html.)

Page 74: *"I used to think that technology . . . "*: Gary Wolf, "Steve Jobs: The Next Insanely Great Thing," *Wired*, February 1996; 106, 107.

Page 75: *education, which comes from the Latin* educare . . . : the Oxford English Dictionary gives the root of "educate" as "L. *educat-*, ppl. stem of educare to rear, bring up (children, young animals), related to *educere* to lead forth."

Part II

Page 77: *Sandy Sparks quote:* Peter H. Lewis, "Computers Beware! New Type of Virus Is Loose on the Net," *The New York Times*, September 4, 1995.

Chapter 5

Page 84: *convincing the consumer to pay for upgrades . . . :* Microsoft's upgrade strategy is documented in James Gleick, "Making Microsoft Safe for Capitalism," *The New York Times Magazine*, November 5, 1995.

Page 84: *obsolete in just* two *years:* Anna Griffith, "Rich Pickings on a Shoestring," *The Observer*, November 5, 1995; 15.

Page 84: *by the year 2005 . . . :* Terry Trucco, "Finding Life for an Old Computer," *The New York Times*, March 23, 1995.

Page 86: *"We see a training gap . . . "*: "Oracle to Make Education a Core Business," Reuters, July 15, 1996.

Page 86: *Americans feel they are losing control:* line is cribbed from Michael J. Sandel, "America's Search for a New Public Philosophy," *The Atlantic Monthly,* March 1996; 57–58

Page 87: *"You can get an optical disk . . . ":* William H. Honan, "At The National Archives, Technology Has a Flip Side," *The New York Times,* October 1, 1995.

Chapter 6

Page 89: *Jane E. Brody quote:* Jane E. Brody, "Personal Health," *The New York Times,* May 18, 1989.

Page 89: *Paralysis by Analysis:* term comes from Richard A. Kuehn, *Business Communications Review,* December 1994.

Page 90: *our court system is inherently antitechnical by design:* Neil Postman points out that our legal structures are heavily relied on these days because they provide an effective antidote to information glut. Neil Postman, *Technopoly* (New York: Vintage, 1993); 73.

Page 90: *"Frye rule":* Kenneth R. Foster, David E. Bernstein, Peter W. Huber, "Science and the Toxic Tort; New Guidelines for the Admissibility of Scientific Evidence," *Science,* September 17, 1993.

Page 90: *"How are we supposed to know this . . . ":* "Supreme Court Considers Rules of Scientific Evidence," *All Things Considered,* March 30, 1993.

Page 91: *"volleys of data":* Richard L. Berke, "Volley's of Data Replace Blatant Attacks of 1988," *The New York Times,* October 29, 1992.

Page 91: *"Much of the Congressional battle . . . ":* Steven Greenhouse, "Seeing Figures, 2 Sides Calculate Clinton's Math," *The New York Times,* February 22, 1993. Other examples of this include:

1. Steven Mufson and David Maraniss, "Candidates Trade Variety of Charges; Some True, Some Misleading, Others Are Simply Obscure," *The Washington Post,* October 20, 1992.

2. Elisabeth Rosenthal, "Claims and Counterclaims on Vaccine Costs Generate Heat but Little Light," *The New York Times,* March 15, 1993.

Page 92: *"bring together into close juxtaposition . . . ":* H. G. Wells, *World Brain* (London: Adadmintine Press, 1994); 89. (From http://wire.co.uk/trendmonitor/wb0.htm.)

Page 92: *"If you don't have some level of confusion . . . ":* National Public Radio, *All Things Considered,* April 13, 1994.

Page 93: *"Is this a sensible situation? . . . ":* Charles C. Mann, "Can Meta-

Analysis Make Policy? Use of Meta-Analysis in the Social Sciences," *Science,* November 11, 1994; 960.

Page 93: *meta-analysis:* Lawrence K. Altman, "New Method of Analyzing Health Data Stirs Debate," *The New York Times,* August 21, 1990.

Page 93: *"controversial method that has provoked dispute . . . ":* Mann, "Can Meta-Analysis Make Policy?" 960.

Page 93: *"You can't choose any one study . . . ":* phone interview, April 6, 1995.

Page 94: *"Clinton carried a lot of information . . . ":* Elizabeth Drew, *On the Edge: The Clinton Presidency* (New York: Simon and Schuster, 1994); 79. (Italics mine.)

Page 94: *"an intense seminar on government minutiae":* Drew, *On the Edge;* 68.

Page 95: *"dataholism":* Ross K. Bake,. "Dataholics Anonymous," *American Demographics,* July 1992. "The obsessive and pathological appetite for data," Baker insists, "is a major new social ill."

Chapter 7

Page 97: *It sounds like it's constructed . . . ":* "What Do the Budget Numbers Really Mean?" National Public Radio, *Morning Edition,* June 23, 1993.

Page 97: *"stat wars":* Michael Kinsley, "Stat Wars," *The New Republic,* March 26, 1990.

Page 97: *"Facts can manipulate and mislead":* Daniel H. Pink, "Year of the Factoid," *The New York Times,* October 29, 1992; 27.

Page 98: *From CNN's* Crossfire: July 16, 1993.

Page 99: *"In the Washington swirl . . . ":* Gregg Easterbrook, "Ideas Move Nations," *The Atlantic Monthly,* January 1986.

Page 99: *"We're not here to be some kind of Ph.D. committee . . . ":* Easterbrook, "Ideas Move Nations."

Page 99: *"conservative commentators have their liberal counterparts out-gunned . . . ":* Easterbrook, "Ideas Move Nations."

Chapter 8

Page 103: *"grabs her ass!":* CBS's *Bless This House.* "What You Can Hear on TV This Fall," *The Indianapolis Star,* August 30, 1995; C1.

Page 103: *San Francisco radio station offers a case of Snapple:* "Dubious Achievement Awards of 1995!" *Esquire,* January 1996; 46.

Page 104: *shock jocks:* Marshall Fine, "Stern's Grip on No. 1 Slips a Bit," *USA Today,* January 16, 1995; 4D. "Stern began simulcasting his New York–based show in 1986. Since then, other radio personalities—including Don Imus, Rick Dees, and Doug "Greaseman" Tracht—have jumped into the syndication game."

Page 104: *"the normalization of hyperbole":* Michael Janofsky, "Increasingly, Political War of Words Is Fought with Nazi Imagery," *The New York Times,* October 23, 1995.

Page 104: *"Everybody knows there's hyperbole in election campaigns":* Neil A. Lewis, "Negative Campaigning on Trial," *The New York Times,* February 25, 1996.

Page 105: *"goose-stepping Gestapo":* Janofsky, "Increasingly, Political War of Words Is Fought with Nazi Imagery."

Page 105: *Anne Fox:* Janofsky, "Increasingly, Political War of Words Is Fought with Nazi Imagery."

Page 105: *Charles Rangel:* Janofsky, "Increasingly, Political War of Words Is Fought with Nazi Imagery."

Page 105: *National Rifle Association:* Janofsky, "Increasingly, Political War of Words Is Fought with Nazi Imagery."

Page 105: *Johnnie Cochran:* Janofsky, "Increasingly, Political War of Words Is Fought with Nazi Imagery."

Page 105: *advertising spending per capita has increased by 2,200 percent:* Jorge Reina Schement and Terry Curtis, *Tendencies and Tensions of the Information Age* (New Brunswick: Transaction Publishers, 1995); 180. (Eli M. Noam, "Visions of the Media Age: Taming the Information Monster," in *Multimedia: A Revolutionary Challenge.* Third Annual Colloquium, June 16/17, 1995 [Frankfurt am Main: Schaffer-Poeschel Verlag Stuttgart, 1995]; 28.)

Page 105: *polls have shown a steep decline in message recall:* In 1986, 64 percent could name a commercial they had seen in the previous four weeks. In 1990 only 48 percent could do so. Mark Plandler, "What Happened to Advertising?" *Business Week,* September 23, 1991; 77–82. (Noam, "Visions of the Media Age"; 28.)

Page 106: *In the 1980s, junk mail grew thirteen times faster than population growth:* Jeff Davidson, *Business and Society Review* 83, September 22, 1992; 4. (Noam, "Visions of the Media Age"; 23.)

Page 106: *"There was a time when people would get very little other than personal mail . . . ":* David Shenk, "Pushing the Envelope," *Spy,* March/April 1996.

Page 107: "Group Warns of Worldwide Water Crisis," Rudy Abramson, *The Los Angeles Times,* November 15, 1992; A, 1:3.

"America's Energy Crisis Beyond the Persian Gulf," David Morrison, *The Atlanta Constitution,* September 26, 1990; A, 13:2

"Crisis Spurs Calls for Auto Mileage Gains," Thomas W. Lippman, *The Washington Post,* August 23, 1990; C, 1:6

"Japan's Environmental 'Time Bombs'," Michael Berger, *The San Francisco Chronicle,* December 24, 1990; A, 1:1

"Pope Warns of Global Ecological Crisis," William D. Montalbano, *The Los Angeles Times* December 6, 1989; A, 6:1

"Report Warns of Trash Crisis, Urges Recycling, Area Planning," Christine Bertelson, *The St. Louis Post-Dispatch,* April 8, 1989; A, 3:4.

"Timber Officials Warn of Economic Crisis," Jamie Beckett, *The San Francisco Chronicle,* January 20, 1989; B1.

Page 107: *more"outrageous" illustrations:* Dan Wasserman, "The Undressing of Everyman," *The Boston Globe,* March 20, 1994; 67.

Page 107: *"When my husband says to someone . . . ":* "Southern California Voices," *The Los Angeles Times,* June 14, 1993; B4.

Page 107: *"We can't go back and put* Ozzie & Harriet *on . . . ":* *The Boston Herald,* November 26, 1995.

Chapter 9

Page 110: *NBA, Toyota, Coca-Cola stats:* Mitchell Stephens, "Pop Goes the World," *The Los Angeles Times Magazine,* January 17, 1993; 22.

Page 111: *hundreds of niche magazines . . . :* Deirdre Carmody, "For Leading Magazines, a Newsstand Slump," *The New York Times,* December 6, 1993. (John M. Harrington, president of the council for periodical distributors associations, says that in 1982 there were 1,800 magazines. In 1993 it was up to 3,300.)

Page 111: *"Virtual communities . . . ":* Bonnie Fisher, Michael Margolis, David Resnick, "A New Way of Talking Politics: Democracy on the Internet," a report presented at the annual meeting of the American Political Science Association in New York City, September 1–4, 1994.

Page 112: *"There's really no mass media left":* Advertising insider Eugene DeWitt. Stats and quote from *Forbes,* September 17, 1980. (In 1978 ABC,

CBS, and NBC had 90 percent of TV viewing audience during prime time. By 1989 that figure was down to 64 percent.)

Page 113: *"[As] the role of each medical practitioner logically narrows . . . ":* Judith A. Sutin, M.D. "Sexual Medicine, Cardiology," *JAMA* 264, July 25, 1990; 526. (There is currently a total of seventy-two subspecialties recognized by the American Board of Medical Specialties.)

Page 114: *"can deliver a lot less geo waste":* Jon Nordheimer, "Cable Becomes New Player in Political Ad Game," *The New York Times,* November 3, 1992.

Page 114: *"Systematic consumer segmentation and 'micro-marketing' . . . ":* John Goss, "We Know Who You Are and We Know Where You Live: The Instrumental Rationality of Geodemographic Systems," *Economic Geography,* April 1995.

Page 115: *ENIAC's size:* Robert E. Calem, *The New York Times* on the Web, February 14, 1996.

Page 115: *UNIVAC:* UNIVAC was commissioned in 1946 and delivered the Census Bureau in 1951, but not put to full use until the 1960 census. Erik Larson, *The Naked Consumer: How Our Private Lives Become Public Commodities* (New York: Penguin, 1992); 36–37.

Page 115: *"human ecologist":* Human ecology applies scientific principles to the study of humans as social beings.

Page 116: *"I reduced something like a billion . . . ":* phone interview conducted by John Arbo, on behalf of the author, May 21, 1996.

Page 116: *Molalla, Oregon . . . :* Michael J. Weiss, *The Clustering of America* (New York: Harper & Row, 1989).

Page 119: *"Pollster Peter Hart . . . ":* phone interview.

Page 120: *gun metaphor:* taken from *Campaigns & Elections* magazine.

Page 120: *"Geodemographics display . . . ":* Goss, "We Know Who You Are."

Page 120: *"Once you make a form of communication . . . ":* Bill Gates, *The Road Ahead* (New York: Viking, 1995); 66, 67.

Chapter 10

Page 123: *Nietzsche quote:* F. W. Nietzsche, "Thus Spake Zarathustra," *The Complete Works of Friedrich Nietzsche,* vol. 2 (London: T. N. Foulis, 1909); 301–6. (Eli M. Noam, "Visions of the Media Age: Taming the Information Monster," in *Multimedia: A Revolutionary Challenge.* Third Annual

Colloquium, June 16/17, 1995 [Frankfurt am Main: Schaffer-Poeschel Verlag Stuttgart, 1995]; 30).

Page 123: *"Of course we're becoming more fragmented . . . ":* Carol Agus Woodier.

Page 125: *Earl Shorris quote:* Earl Shorris, "The Novelist and the Normal World," *The New York Times,* July 1, 1984.

Page 125: *"IBM InfoSage":* from a letter sent to consumers in May 1996.

Page 126: *Reader's Digest:* Michael J. Weiss, *The Clustering of America* (New York: Harper & Row, 1989); 27.

Page 126: *"Over the last three decades . . . ":* James Fallows, *Breaking the News: How the Media Undermine Democracy* (New York: Pantheon, 1996); 68.

Page 128: *"If the answer is never . . . ":* Bill Bradley, speaking at Center for National Policy, October 1993, quoted in Michael Kelly, "A Sense of Where He's Going," *The New Yorker,* March 6, 1995.

Page 129: *"Leadership is harder . . . ":* Robert Wright, "Hyperdemocracy," *Time,* January 23, 1995; 14.

Page 129: *We need shared discourse to support our pluralistic culture:* In a conversation (May 7, 1996) with the author, Eli Noam issued a rebuttal to this point. Noam's view of the world is more Hegelian, wherein this faction and that faction are always in conflict. They regularly bring their disagreements to a parliament, which is trained to come to a compromise. Whereas Shenk's view is that when factions can't understand each other, society suffers, Noam sees society as competing interests that get along *only* through a form of civil strife. From this perspective, specialization isn't so bad. It only increases the communication efficiency within each special interest group. (Either way, we agree that specialization does portend the near-extinction of the Statesman, the generalist, who is able to put society-splintered perspectives into one grand unifying perspective.)

Chapter 11

Page 131: *Umberto Eco quote:* Umberto Eco, "Ur–Fascism," *The New York Review of Books,* June 22, 1995. (Thanks to Jack Kessler, via the list pacs-l@uhupvm1.uh.edu.)

Page 131: *Stryker is not the first to suggest . . . :* Over the course of this century, direct democracy has garnered a small but dedicated following, along with a slew of monikers: "Computocracy," "Video Democracy," "Real Democracy," "Telecommunitarian Democracy," "Electronic Town

Meeting," and so on. "We have outlived the historical usefulness of representative democracy," declares John Naisbitt in *Megatrends,* summing up the thoughts of a disparate band of techno-enthusiasts. "We have grown more confident of our own ability to make decisions about how institutions, including government and corporations, should operate." John Naisbitt, *Megatrends* (New York: Warner Books, 1984); 177.

Page 132: *Perot on electronic town hall:* Michael Kelly, "The 1992 Campaign: Third-Party Candidate. Perot's Vision: Consensus by Computer," *The New York Times,* June 6, 1992.

Page 132: *"You come home . . . ":* "Superdemocracy," Tim Stryker. *Telecomputing,* November 1990.

Page 133: *Congressional mail:* Eli M. Noam, "Visions of the Media Age: Taming the Information Monster," in *Multimedia: A Revolutionary Challenge.* Third Annual Colloquium, June 16/17, 1995 (Frankfurt am Main: Schaffer-Poeschel Verlag Stuttgart, 1995); 20–24.

Page 134: *"Almost every American . . . ":* Robert Wright, "Hyperdemocracy," *Time,* January 23, 1995; 14.

Page 134: *consortium of long-distance phone companies:* David Segal, "Telecommunications Legislation Sparks a Storm on the Hill; Legislators Challenge Telegrams' Credibility," *The Washington Post,* August 4, 1995; B1.

Page 135: *"probably as high as they have ever been":* "Some Aspire to Greatness," *The Economist,* April 16, 1994; 32. (See also: Scott Shepard, "Decline in Respect Hampers Congress in Job, Experts Say," *The Atlanta Journal and Constitution,* June 10, 1994.)

Page 135: *"What's the Senate's chief concern . . . ":* "Senate May Call for U.S. Troop Withdrawal from Somalia," National Public Radio, *Morning Edition,* October 14, 1993.

Page 136: *"The scientific methodology of contemporary opinion . . . ":* Suzannah Lessard, "Banish the Pollsters," *The Washington Monthly,* January/February 1996; 26.

Page 137: *Government is all* too responsive . . . : Point buttressed by Jonathan Schell, "The Debt and the Demons of August," *Newsday,* October 18, 1992; 29. "What if the politicians, far from being out of touch with the people, were in fact all too closely in touch? What if, as was the case here, they had been paying hundreds of thousands of dollars year in and year out for polls, focus groups and so forth, precisely in order to monitor every nuance of the people's will, and had fashioned most of the major policies of government with a view to satisfying that will, whether or not those policies, in the view of budget directors and the like, made sense? Is there in fact the tiniest shred of evidence that the fault of the candidates who won high office in the 1980s and in 1990 has been inattention to the opinions of the public? Public-opinion polls, whose results are the very currency of power in late 20th-Century United States, are these politicians' oracles and deities. None of which is to suggest, of course, that the politicians have been the altruistic servants of the people. The point is that their own chief self-interest—getting into power and staying there—lies precisely in staying as closely in touch with public opinion as possible."

Part III

Page 139: *"Whether it's about agency billings . . . "*: editorial, "Defining Disinformation Dispensers," *Advertising Age,* October 20, 1986; 17.

Chapter 12

Page 142: *nonstandard Egyptian hieroglyphs . . . :* David Kahn, *The Codebreakers* (New York: Macmillan, 1967); 71.

Page 142: *away from the eyes of the IRS:* Dan Lehrer, "Clipper Chips and Cypherpunks," *The Nation,* October 10, 1994.

Page 143: *largest electronic petition in history . . . :* Luke Seemann, "The Clipper Chip and Key Escrow Encryption," http://www.stardot.com/~lukeseem/j202/essay.html.

Chapter 13

Page 145: *McDonald's manager:* Pamela Mendels, "$2M Suit in Sweet Nuthin' Eavesdrop," *Newsday,* January 20, 1995; A4.

Page 145: *I don't like that lead!:* Gene Bylinsky, "How Companies Spy on Employees," *Fortune,* November 4, 1991; 131.

Page 145: *Ron Edens:* Tony Horwitz, "Mr. Edens Profits from Watching His Workers' Every Move," *The Wall Street Journal,* December 1, 1994; 9.

Page 146: *"Our smallest actions leave digital trails . . . ":* Nicholas Negroponte, "Double Agents," *Wired,* March 1995; 172.

Page 146: *"Marketers should take full advantage . . . ":* Eric Clark, *The Want Makers* (New York: Viking, 1988); 64.

Page 147: *"In the great scheme of things . . . ":* Judith Waldrop, "The Business of Privacy," *American Demographics,* October 1994; 46.

Page 147: *the CD-ROM would have made the information much more affordable . . . :* Frank V. Cespedes and H. Jeff Smith, "Database Marketing: New Rules for Policy and Practice," *Sloan Management Review,* June 22, 1993; 7.

Page 147: *After the MarketPlace implosion, the rest of the industry let out an audible sigh of relief:* Waldrop, "The Business of Privacy."

Page 148: *companies to cultivate a massive collection of detailed personal data . . . : Redbook,* October 1992.

Page 148: *Lotus's major mistake:* The CD-ROM, lamented Lotus CEO Jim Manzi, was "at the apex of an emotional firestorm of public concern about consumer privacy." Lawrence M. Fisher, "New Data Base Ended By Lotus and Equifax," *The New York Times,* January 24, 1991; D4.

Page 148: *mounting resentment against the loss of privacy . . . :* M. A. Stapleton, "Information Age, Sans Safeguards, Could Become Information Cage," *The Chicago Daily Law Bulletin,* April 27, 1996. (Further evidence: A public opinion survey by Louis Harris & Associates in 1993 found that 83 percent of Americans are concerned about threats to their personal privacy, a 5 percentage point increase from the year before and a 49 point increase from a similar poll conducted in 1970.)

Page 148: *Snow Crash:* Neal Stephenson, *Snow Crash* (New York: Bantam Books, 1993); 394–95.

Page 149: *"Twenty minutes ago, Jake Lamb . . . ":* Clark, *The Want Makers;* 59, 60.

Page 149: *Dr. Sidney Weinstein:* Clark, *The Want Makers;* 59, 60.

Page 150: *"The answers they give . . . ":* Clark, *The Want Makers;* 61.

Page 150: *"It's a whole new dimension for us . . . ":* James Atlas, "Beyond Demographics," *The Atlantic Monthly,* October 1984.

Page 150: *BehaviorScan:* Alexander Star, *The New Republic,* February 15, 1993. ("Science of consumption" is Star's phrase.)

Page 151: *DejaNews Partners:* Stapleton, "Information Age, Sans Safeguards."

Page 151: *Educational Testing Service: Redbook,* October 1992.

Page 151: *Goebbels quote:* Anthony Pratkanis, Elliot Aronson, *Age of Propaganda* (New York: W. H. Freeman, 1992); 49.

Page 152: *Spinoza:* phone interview with Gilbert.

Chapter 14

Page 156: *has appeared on the "nonfiction" New York Times bestseller book list . . . :* Timothy Egan, "Chief's Speech of 1854 Given New Meaning (and Words)," *The New York Times,* April 21, 1992; 1. (*Brother Eagle, Sister Sky: A Message from Chief Seattle* was number five on *The New York Times* bestseller list for nonfiction.)

Page 156: *"It's a classic case . . . ":* Egan, "Chief's Speech of 1854."

Page 157: *"The anecdote—selective, exaggerated, or just wrong . . . ":* Daniel Schorr, "Political Anecdotes Often Have Little Basis in Truth," National Public Radio, *All Things Considered,* March 6, 1995.

Page 157: *anecdotage:* William Safire, "Ten Myths About the Reagan Debacle," *The New York Times Magazine,* March 22, 1987; 21.

Page 157: *too many sweets:* thanks to Mitch Stephens for this metaphor.

Page 157: *"Without metaphor, thought . . . ":* Frank Smith, *Essays into Literacy* (Portsmouth, NH: Heinemann Press, 1983); 117.

Page 157: *"welfare queen":* Schorr, "Political Anecdotes Often Have Little Basis in Truth." (More on the welfare queen: Blaine Harden, *The Washington Post,* May 2, 1982.)

Page 158: *"We suppose that if you persist . . . ":* editorial, "An Act of Cynicism," *The Washington Post,* September 9, 1981.

Page 158: *Drug bust in Lafayette Park:* Joe Frolik, "Drug War Dwindles to Skirmish," *The Times-Picayune,* March 6, 1994; A1.

Page 158: *"I'd put it in evolutionary terms . . . ":* phone interview with Richard Nisbett, April 19, 1995.

Page 158: *subjects were introduced to a prison guard . . . :* Nisbett.

Page 159: *"Bush Encounters the Supermarket . . . ":* Andrew Rosenthal, "Bush Encounters the Supermarket, Amazed," *The New York Times,* February 5, 1992; 1.

Page 160: *Exhibit A:* "It hurt the president badly . . . ": Marlin Fitzwater, *Call The Briefing: Reagan & Bush, Sam & Helen. A Decade of Presidents* (New York: Times Books, 1995); 328.

Page 160: *Exhibit B:* "Credibility Gap in 'Hairgate,'" *The Louisville Courier-Journal,* July 4, 1993; 4D. (Excerpted from a *Newsday* editorial.)

Page 161: *Exhibit C:* Sam Roberts, "Famous Line Was 'Quiet.' Not 'Shut Up,'" *The New York Times,* October 26, 1993.

Page 161: *"Double-Blind trials demonstrated that branding . . . ":* Judie

Lannon, Peter Cooper, *International Journal of Advertising,* 1983. (From Clark, *The Want Makers;* 207–8.)

Chapter 15

Page 163: *"Tomorrow's communications . . . ":* James M. Alexander and James E. Lukaszewski, "Virtual PR Nears Reality," *J. R. O'Dwyer Co., Inc. PR Services,* January 1995.

Page 164: *"Though these programs can look like Discovery Channel documentaries . . . ":* Thomas Goetz, "I'm Not a Reporter; But I Play One on GOP-TV," *The Columbia Journalism Review,* September 1994. Anne Gavin, spokeswoman for the Republican National Committee's GOP-TV: "Our aim is to bypass the media elite with our message."

Page 164: *A number of new investment magazines like* MoneyWorld, . . . : Duff McDonald, "Some Financial Magazines Arriving in Your Mailbox May Well Be Phonies," *Money,* October 1996; 24.

Page 164: *"We saw this as a hugely added value":* Robin Pogrebin, "The Number of Ad Pages Does Not Make the Magazine," *The New York Times,* August 26, 1996; D1.

Page 165: *advertorials in the school classroom:* David Shenk, "Investing in Our Youth," *Spy,* July/August 1994.

Page 165: *"Why should the media be allowed to filter your message anyway? . . . ":* Jack O'Dwyer, "Revolution Has Started," *Jack O'Dwyer's Newsletter,* February 22, 1995; 3.

Page 165: *"give the news, all the news . . . ":* *The New York Times,* August 19, 1896. (From *The Newseum News History Content Book,* fourth draft, August 1995. Freedom Forum Newseum, Arlington, Virginia.)

Page 167: *social glue:* thanks to Nancy Woodhull and Nancy Maynard at the Freedom Forum Media Studies Center.

Page 167: *a bypassed media would be a disaster:* "Journalism has functioned for generations as a national information wellhead," says media critic Jon Katz. Now, he warns, "the wellhead is beginning to come apart, threatening an anarchic void." Jon Katz, "Bulletin Boards: News from Cyberspace," *Rolling Stone,* April 15, 1993.

Page 167: *"[Newspapers are] that universal circulation . . . ":* Arthur Young, *Travels During the Years 1787, 1788, and 1789* (1792). Referenced in Harold A. Innis, *Empire and Communications* (Toronto: University of Toronto Press, 1972).

Page 168: *"My job is not to educate the public . . . ":* Richard Heffner, host of "The Open Mind," August 8, 1993.

Page 170: *"In the '20s and '30s . . . ":* phone interview.

Page 171: *public journalism:* Davis "Buzz" Merritt, *Public Journalism & Public Life: Why Telling the News is Not Enough* (Hillsdale, New Jersey: Lawrence Erlbaum Associates, Publishers, 1995).

Chapter 16

Page 173: *Thomas:* http://thomas.loc.gov.

Page 173: *"change the balance of power . . . ":* "Access to Electronic Legal Cases Hits a Snag," National Public Radio, *Morning Edition,* January 26, 1995.

Page 174: *"The information age means more decentralization . . . ":* Newt Gingrich, *From Virtuality to Reality,* http://www.pff.org/pff/pff6.html.

Page 174: *Control revolution:* For more on this, see Andrew L. Shapiro, "Freedom from Choice," *Wired,* December 1997; 213; and "Privacy for Sale: Peddling Data on the Internet," *The Nation,* June 23, 1997; 11.

Page 175: *"He 'gets it' . . . ":* Esther Dyson, "Friend and Foe," *Wired,* August 1995; 107–8.

Page 175: *"Magna Carta for the Knowledge Age":* http://www.pff.org/pff/position.html.

Page 175: *PFF claims to be both educational and nonpartisan:* For more on this nonprofit tax dodge, see David Shenk, "Nonprofiteers," *The Washington Monthly,* December 1991; 35–39.

Page 176: *"[The Knowledge Age] will not deliver. . . ":* http://www.pff.org/pff/position.html.

Part IV

Page 179: *Superabundant information is grand:* Dr. Philip Novak, associate professor and chairman, Department of Philosophy and Religious Studies, from commencement address at Dominican College, San Rafael, California, 1988. *Dominican Quarterly,* Summer 1988.

Chapter 17

Page 181: *"Almost anybody can add information . . . ":* Eli M. Noam, "Visions of the Media Age: Taming the Information Monster," in

Multimedia: A Revolutionary Challenge. Third Annual Colloquium, June 16/17, 1995 (Frankfurt am Main: Schaffer-Poeschel Verlag Stuttgart, 1995); 18–19.

Page 182: *Brian Lamb:* lecture at Columbia University, October 17, 1995.

Page 182: *Success on . . . the nutrition front . . . :* Americans are consuming proportionately less fat and saturated fat in the '90s than they were in the late '70s. Advance data from *Vital and Health Statistics* 255, "Energy and Macronutrient Intakes of Persons Ages 2 Months and Over in the United States." Http://www/cdc.gov/nchswww/faq/dietary/htm.

Chapter 18

Page 187: *Michael Dertouzos: Technology Review,* August/September 1994.

Chapter 19

Page 194: *A Prairie Home Companion:* broadcast live on Public Radio International, Saturday evenings, 6 P.M. E.S.T.

Chapter 20

Page 199: *"Expect the downtech movement to grow . . . ":* Hugh Heclo, "Downteching: The Coming Heresy," *The Observer, Columbia University Journal for General Studies* 6, no. 7, April/May 1994; 7.

Page 199: *"To live more simply is to live more purposefully . . . ":* Duane Elgin, *Voluntary Simplicity: Toward a Way of Life That Is Outwardly Simple, Inwardly Rich* (New York: Quill, 1993).

Chapter 21

Page 201: *"If the answer is never, . . . ":* Bill Bradley, speaking at Center for National Policy, October 1993, quoted in Michael Kelly, "A Sense of Where He's Going," *The New Yorker,* March 6, 1995.

Chapter 22

Page 207: *"do-not-disturb" registry:* Actually, a voluntary version of such a registry is already in place, run by the Direct Marketing Association. But in order for this to be taken seriously, it must become compulsory.

Page 208: *"We're sitting, as most cities are . . . ":* Peter Applebome, "How

Atlanta's Adman Pushes the City to Sell Itself," *The New York Times,* February 9, 1993; A16.

Page 209: *The vast majority of Americans are concerned with deception in ads . . . :* from a 1980 study by Yankelovich, Skelly, and White. Michael Schudson, *Advertising, The Uneasy Persuasion* (Basic Books, 1984).

Page 210: *"half truths and motivational manipulations . . . ":* Stanley E. Cohen, *Advertising Age,* March 5, 1984. (From Clark, *The Want Makers;* 128.)

Page 210: *"If we allow the information superhighway to bypass the less fortunate . . . ":* Vice President Al Gore, in a speech at the National Press Club, December 21, 1993.

Page 212: *"It is a lovely process . . . ":* Richard Sclove, Loka Alert 3:4, June 7, 1996, "Town Meetings on Technology," obtained at: http://www.am herst.edu/~loka.

Index

sible editing of, 191–95; on U.S. households, 115–19; widening gap of access to, 210–11. *See also* knowledge

information anxiety, 84–87

information discrepancy, 28–29

"information have-nots," 210–11

information overload: as a genuine threat, 25–26; journalism to filter, 166–67; memory loss due to, 47–49; as number one issue, 29; perception/judgments and, 152–53; personal experiences on, 44–45; solutions to, 185–89, 191–95; as threat to journalism, 167–71; two-by-four effect and, 103–8; urban stress and, 38–40

Information Resources, Inc., 150

information revolution: cultural fragmentation and, 111–21; dark visions of, 141–42; democracy and, 124–25, 131–37; misguided utopian faith in, 60–61, 63–64; overwhelming nature of, 21–24; privacy issues of, 146–48, 209; realities of the, 65–67; stress of, 36; unintended consequences of, 51–56. *See also* technology

"information wants to be free" motto, 92

InfoSage (IBM), 125–26, 188

Internet: advertising on the, 32; classroom connection to the, 73–75; creation of lay media and, 165–66; government and the, 205–13; information fragmentation in the, 125; information overload on the, 25–26; Republican cyberspace of the, 174–78; RISKS forum of, 57; spamming on the, 24–25; utopian fever of the, 72; World Wide Web of, 64, 65, 110, 128

Jamieson, Kathleen Hall, 104

Jefferson, Thomas, 142

Jobs, Steve, 71, 74

Johnson, Samantha, 45

journalism: advertisements disguised as, 164–66; information filtered by good, 166–67; information overload threat to, 167–71; public, 171; tabloidization of, 107. *See also* media

junk e-mail lists, 217–18

junk mail, 106

"junk science" testimony, 90

J. Walter Thompson agency, 161–62

K.'s story, 51–54

Kapor, Mitch, 69

Kay, Alan, 74

Keillor, Garrison, 194

Kennedy, John F., 15

Kerrey, Bob, 97

Kessler, David, 210

Keyworth, George, 175

Kinsley, Michael, 97, 98

knowledge: computers used as tool for, 73–75; political, 66–67, 124–25; power and, 173–74. *See also* information

Kohut, Andrew, 65, 124, 136

Kudzu ecological problem, 54

Lamb, Brian, 21–22, 182

Lamb, Jake, 149, 150

Lapham, Lewis, 20

laws of data smog, 11. *See also* data smog

Lehrer, Brian, 201–2

Lehtonen, Jaako, 28

Leonsis, Ted, 165–66

Lessard, Suzannah, 136

Life magazine, 124

lifestyle analysis, 116–19

Lifetime Learning Systems, 165

Lincoln, Abraham, 113

List-Link law, 48–49

lobbying, 134

long-distance phone companies, 134

Look magazine, 124

Lotus MarketPlace, 147–48